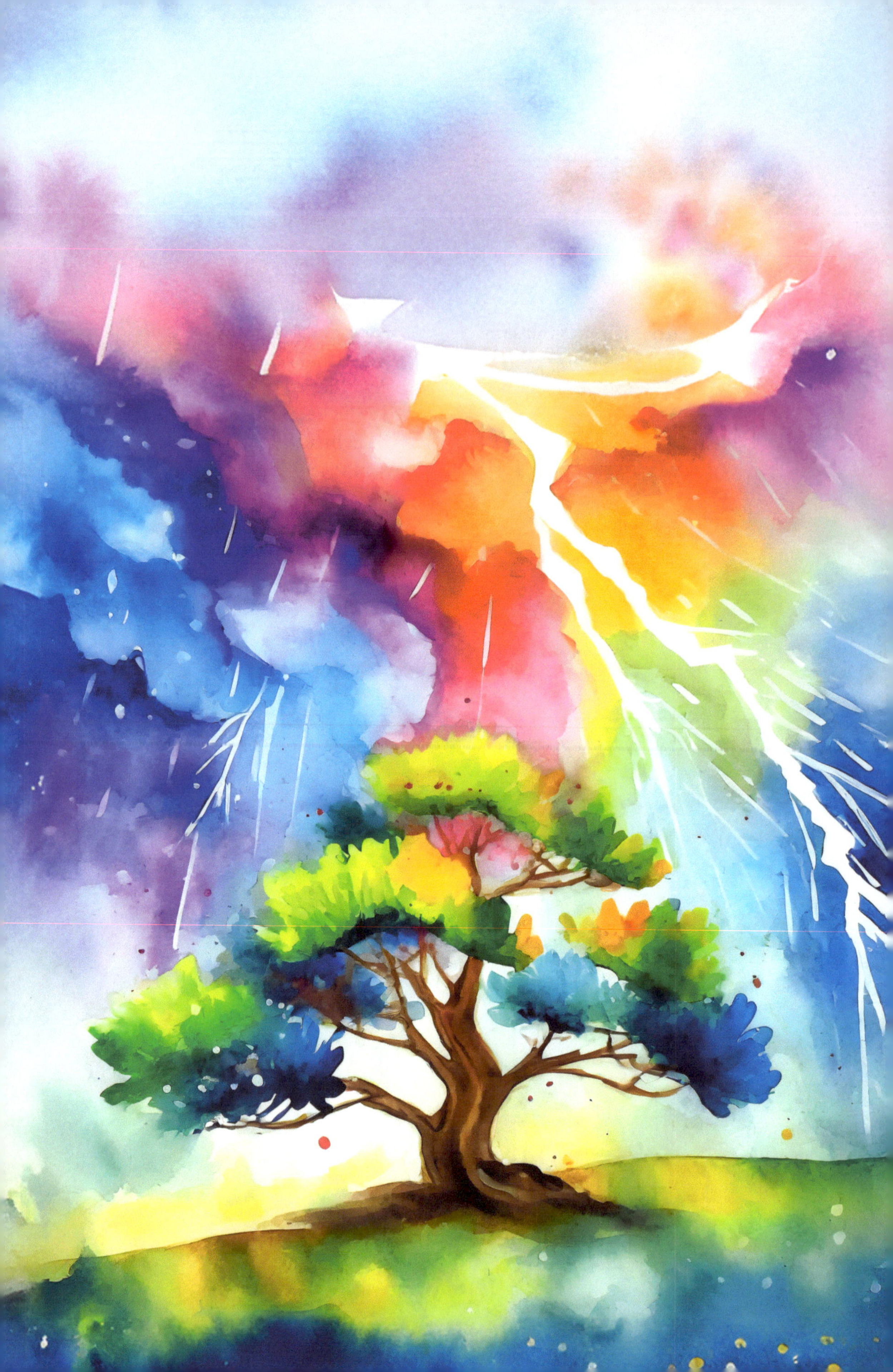

ALIVENESS

It is known
Beyond the eyes the ears
The hands the tongue
It is sensed
Beneath the bones the skin
The blood the cells
The insight remembers
A soul experience
A spiritual existence
Aliveness

SECRET REMEDY

An overactive mind
Aches for more
An underactive heart
Aches for more
An everactive body
Aches and aches
And the secret remedy
To the headache heartache
Back breaking aching
Is in the stillness

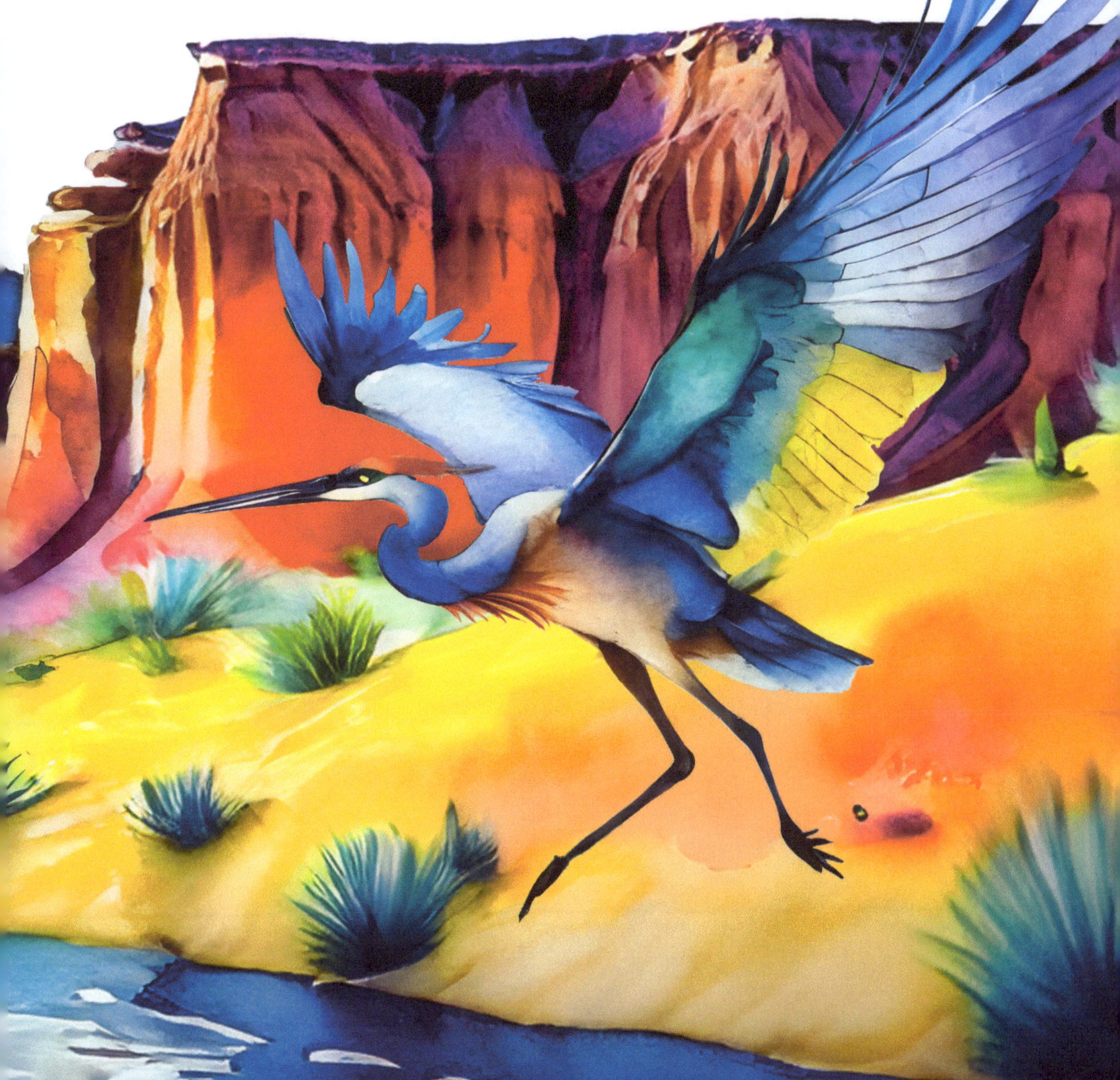

WHAT IS REAL

Your brother the heron
Refuses to fly
At some point in life
Your brother the wild horse
Reduces to a workhorse
Refusing to run
Your brother
The blessed human being
Ensnares himself in the traps
The ego trips
Being a human doing
Stooping to the do do do
As humans do
Always never sometimes—

Still
In the stillness sometimes
Never always magic comfort comes
Miracles bring medicine
To remedy the dis-ease
Mystical powers arrive they arise
To resolve the dis-order
Disempowerment discouragement
Distortion distraction destruction...
Mysteries intervene
Revealing
What is real

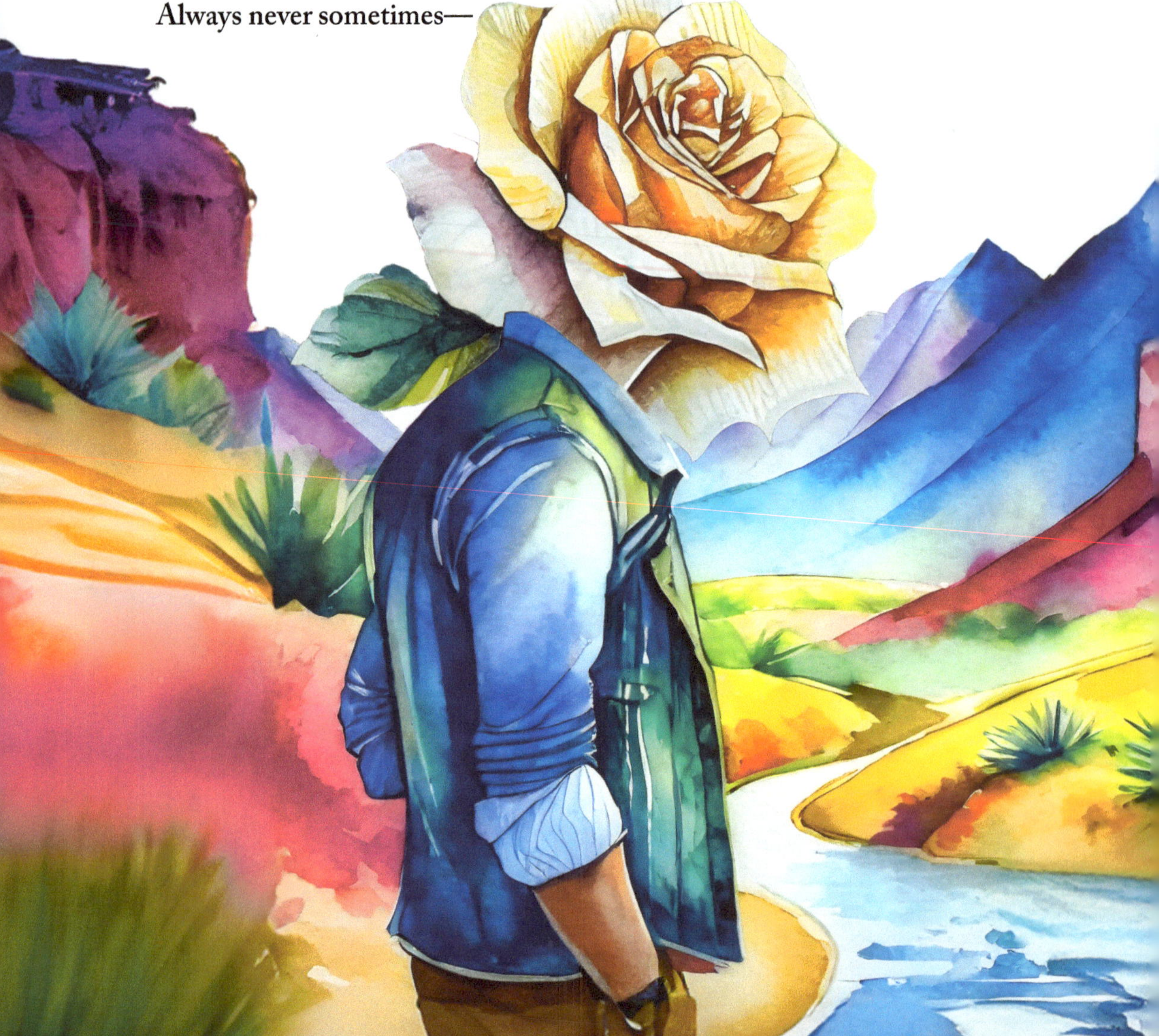

MUSTANG
ONCE

Mustangs must stay
Hidden away
Out in the wild country space
When we wild horses
Leave the mountains
We rarely return the same
I was a mustang until
I left Wyoming
Just to become a workhorse
Just to work like a donkey
I must
Be a mustang
Again
Cowboys and cowmen
Saddle us down
Hammer nails into our hooves
Cowgirls cowwomen
Fence us in
And tell us where to go
I was a mustang until
I left Wyoming
Just to become a workhorse
Just to work like a donkey
I must
Be a mustang again
Broncos bet busted
Stallions get broken
Branded with hot iron
Braided like show ponies
Ridden in polo games
Horse races and rodeos
I was a mustang once
I was a mustang—
Once
I was a mustang until
I left Wyoming
Just to become a workhorse
Just to work like a donkey
I must
Be a mustang again

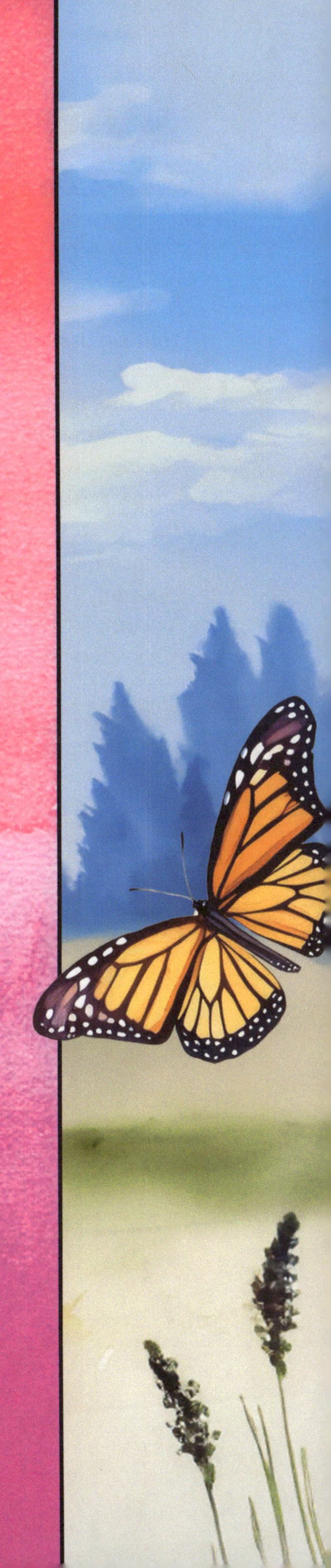

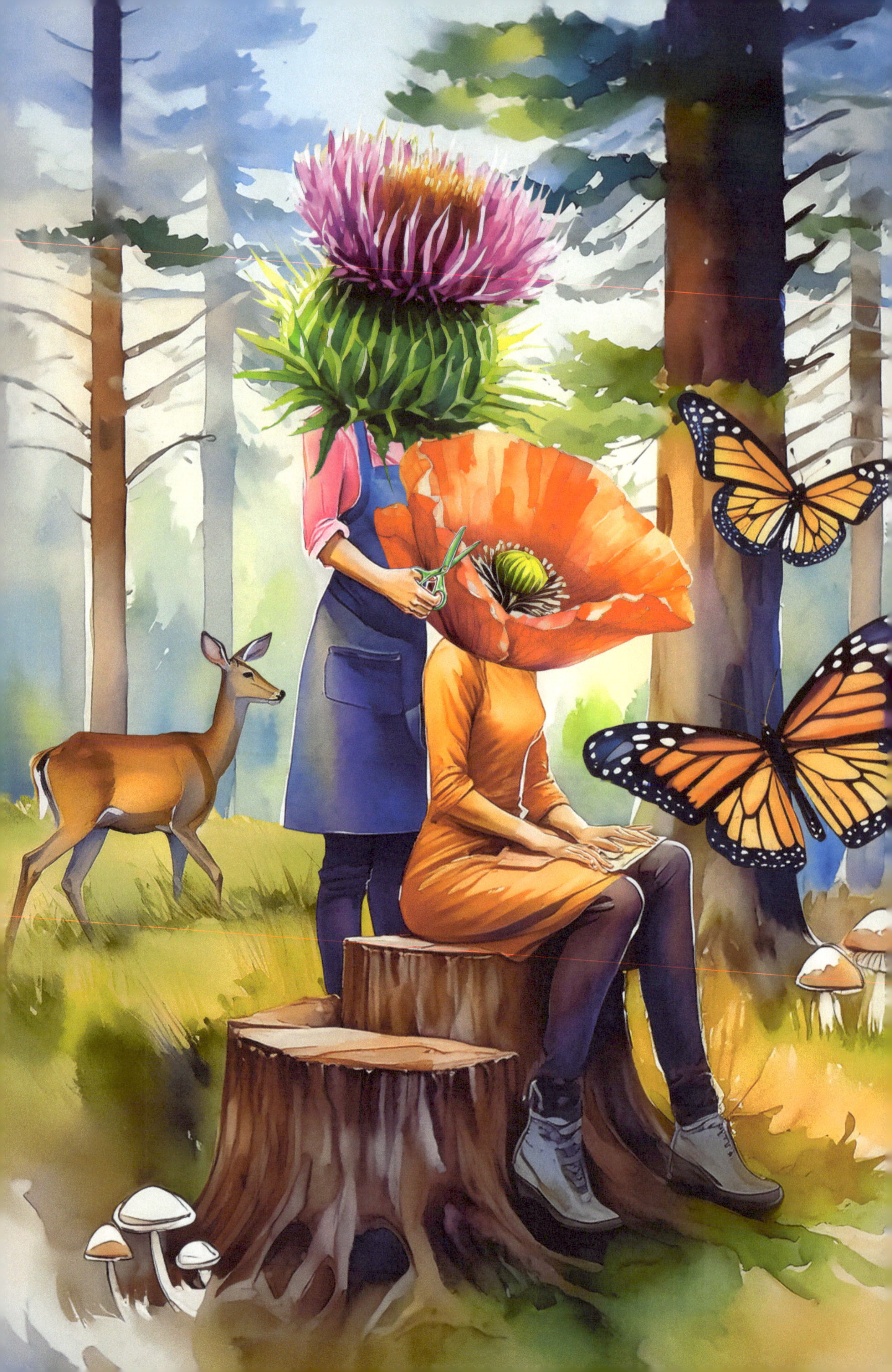

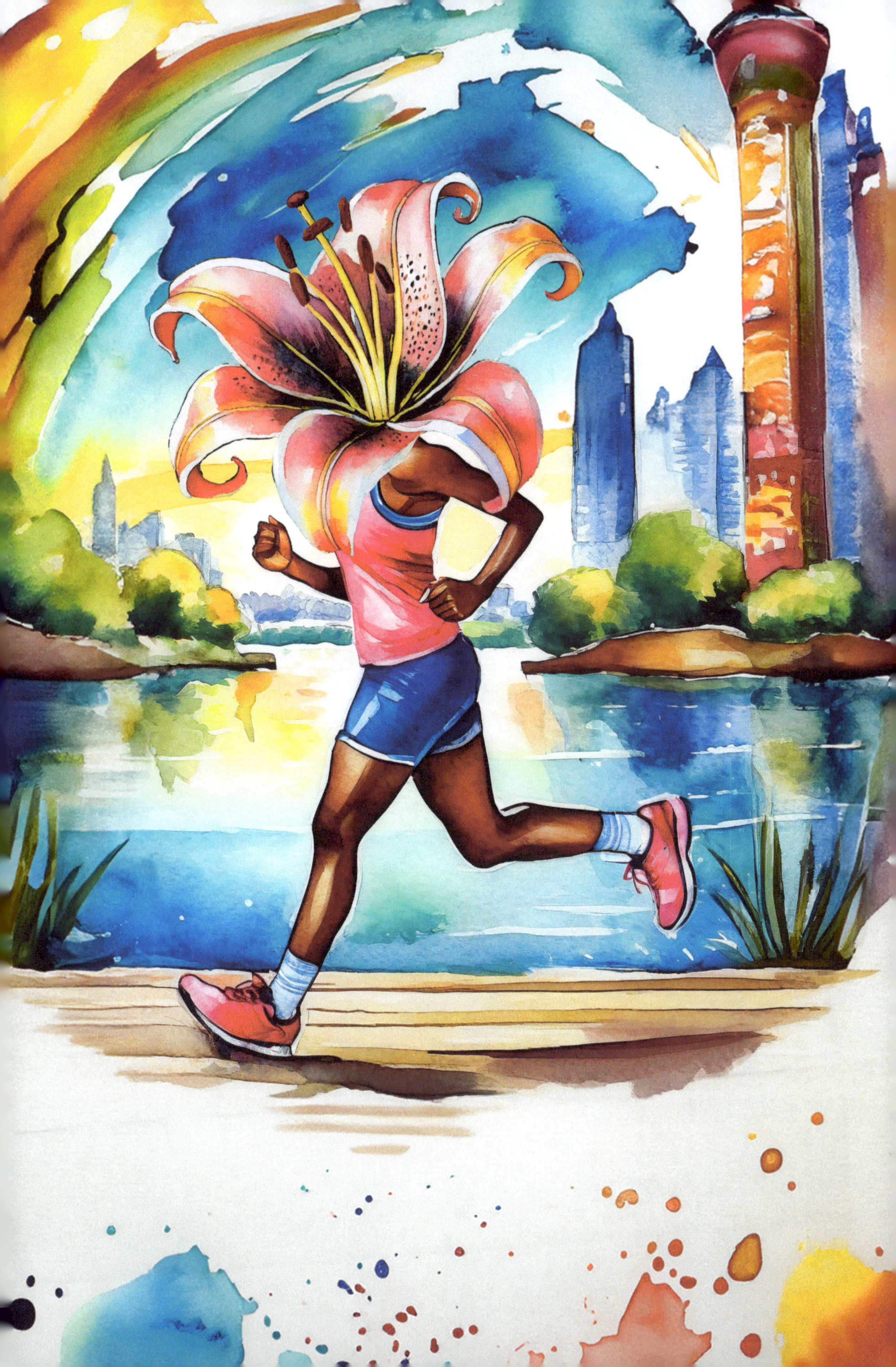

COLLECTING MYSELF

I collect artifacts of the past
Articles of the classics—
Arrowheads fossils crystals
Petrified wood
Skulls snakeskins antlers bones—
Signs of life before life
Symbols of wild existence
Wild death
They inspire me
To leave a legacy
To make my mark on Earth
Just as She gives me
Her heartbeat—
Dune dune dune dune
My heart beats with Her
▷▷▷▷
My heart beats
With Mozart + Vivaldi
Silvio Rodríguez + Billie Holiday
Gabriel García Márquez
Ayn Rand... artists
Of other worlds + olden times
▷▷▷▷
Humbling myself
Waiting for my time to shine
Praying on my knees
Through the night
Thanking the Maker
For making me light as a feather
When I take the talking stick
Recalling my influences
Collecting myself
Kneeling tall
Speaking up
Singing high
All the while—
Dune dune dune dune
My heart beats with Her

LIFT THE VEIL

Wishing to be free
The wolf in me
Wants to howl
But only the wind
Holds that high luxury
In this social scene
So I and my emotions
Go coasting by the ocean
Arriving at sunset
When the time comes
For a fire by the beach
Sparkles bring wonder
Comforting the kids
As waves roll in
Soothing with the songs I sing
▷▷▷▷
The wildflower in me
Learns to flourish
In a world of dirt
Where sky meets sea
Fire meets water
The Sun the moon the stars
Ripple and sway in the waves
Even the humminbird the butterfly
Bathe in the wind fire water earth
I bathe in the space in between
Where the veil separates
Visible from invisible
Audible from inaudible
Head from heart
Soul from flesh and bone—
Always never sometimes
I lift the veil

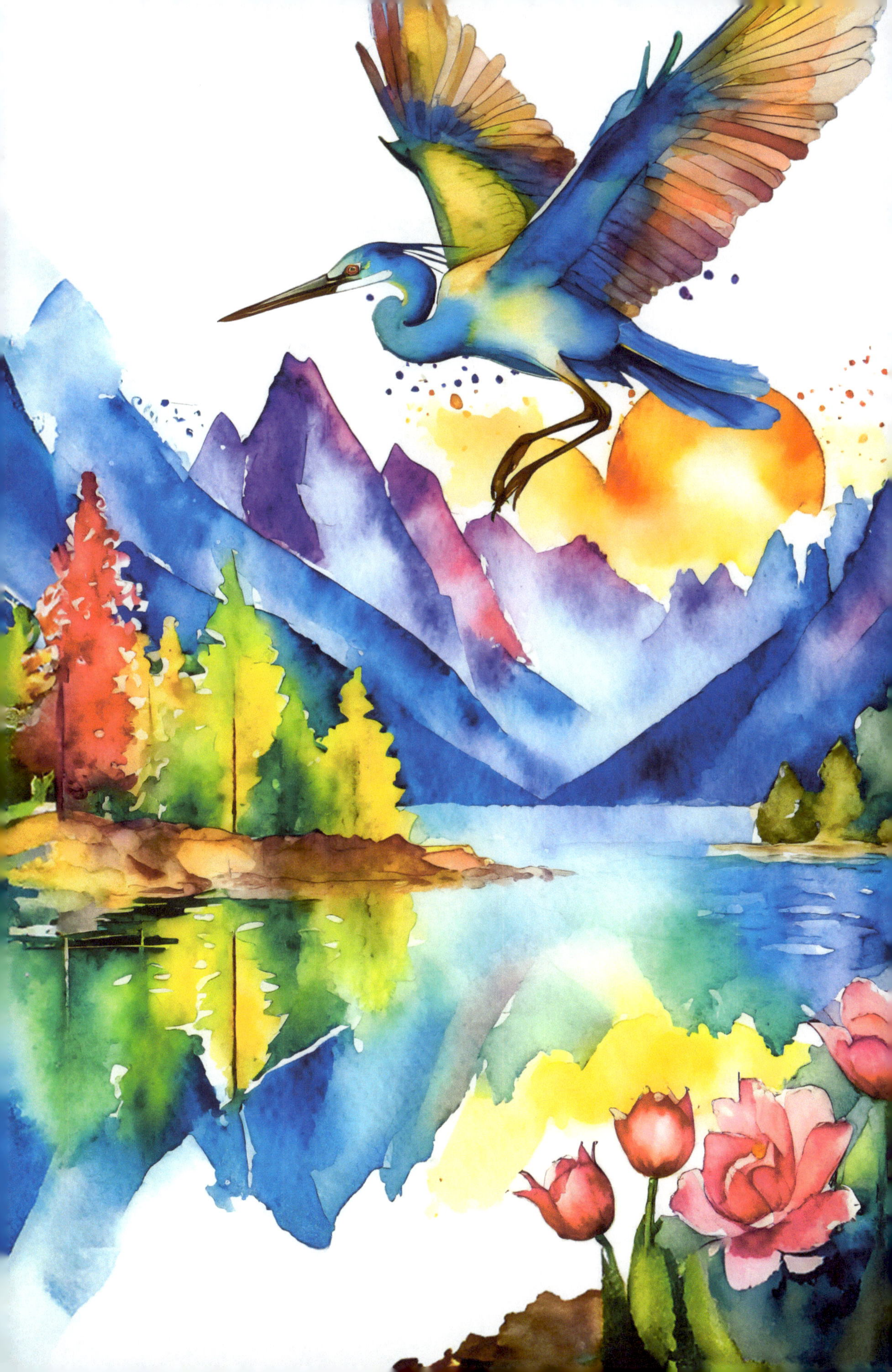

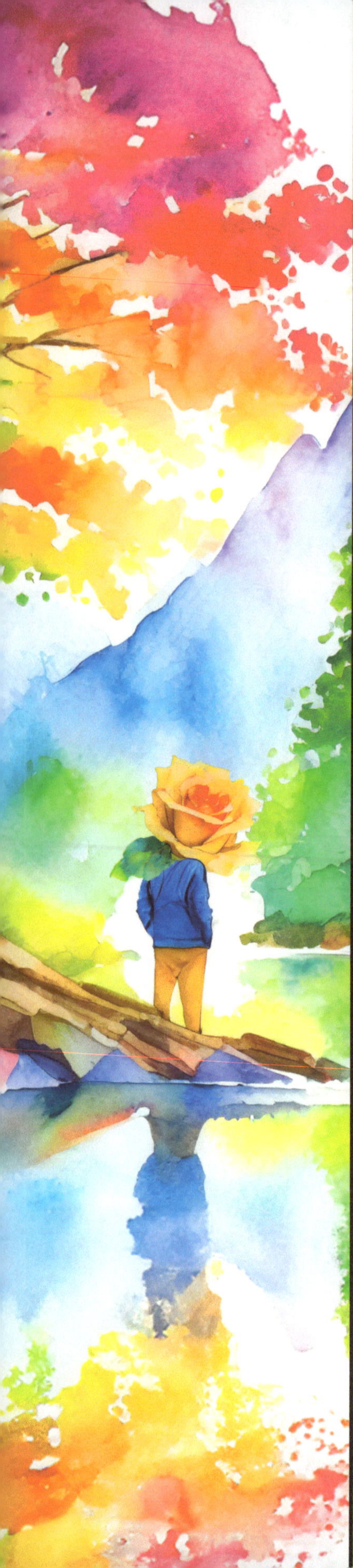

ALONE

Here I am alone
Not because my love leaves me
But because I leave my love
Fearing I'll be left behind
Now I'm upset
Not because I'm fired
But because I quit
Afraid of being freed
Why do I fear my freedom?
Because it forces me to feel to see
To wield wild power—
Willpower
Empowered I fear powerlessness
Here I am possessed
Not because my eyes shine bright
But because I stare at fire
Afraid of being dim dumb numb
Here I am distressed
Not because I can't stop working
But because I won't stop
Fearing the cold loathsome
Loneliness
Of self-obsession
The rigid brittleness
Of depression
▷▷▷▷
Upon reflection
On the murky waters of my worlds
With unknown sinkholes
Beneath a glassy surface
A minnow swims in and out of view
Drawing my attention inward
A smooth stone calls me
To soothing waters of my Innermost
Where I find a riverstone to throw—
Skipping ripples show
A graceful way to make my mark
Willflower
A waterbird wades
In gentle waves

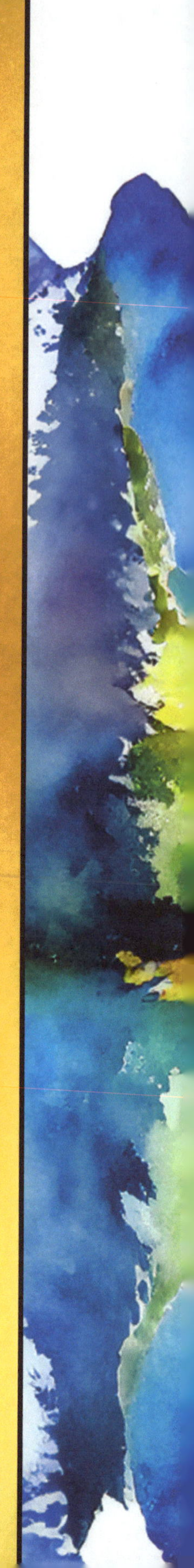

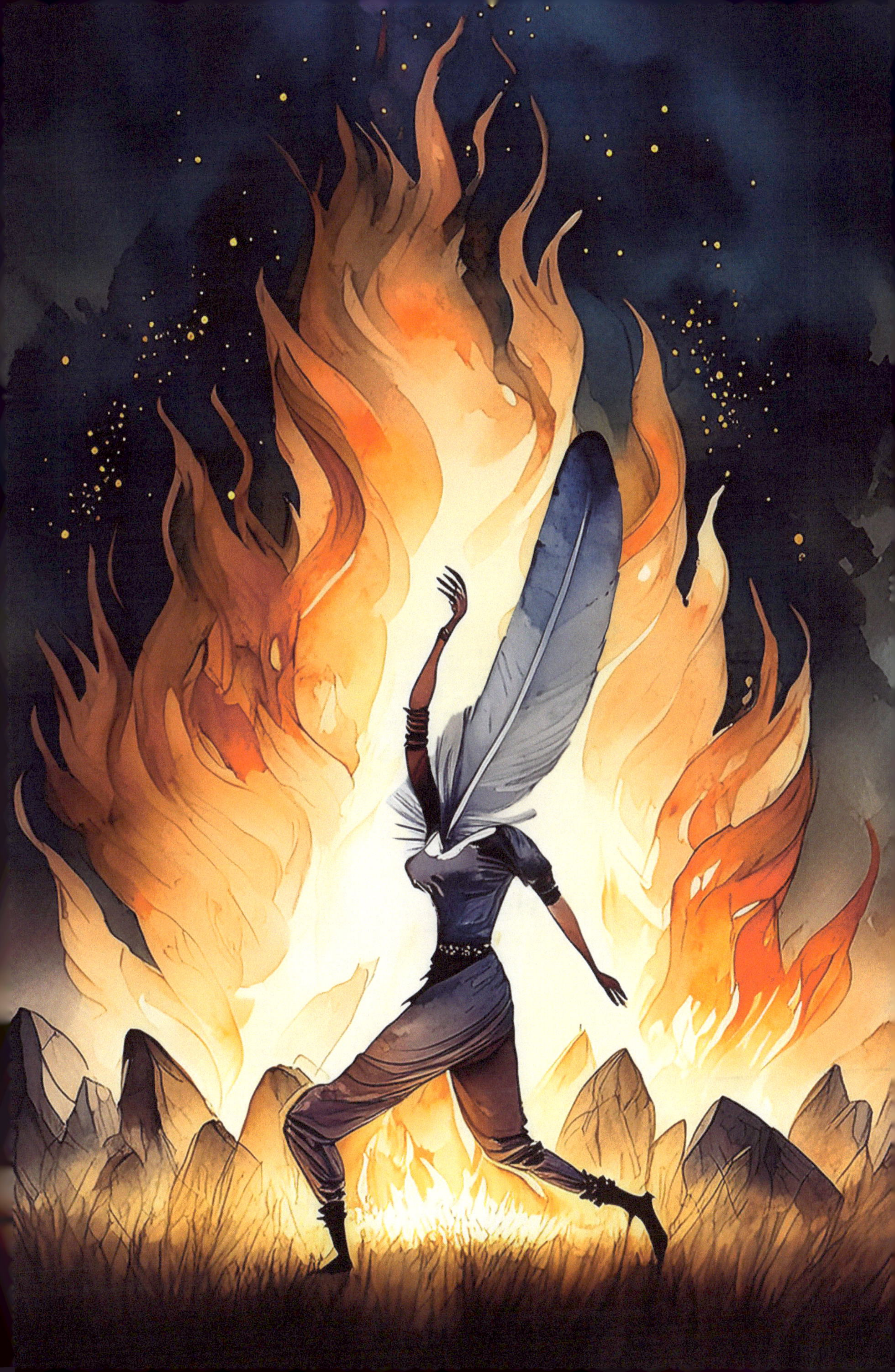

ENERGY KNOWS

Fire inside
Drives us outside
Showing corridors
Through the unknown
Energy knows
Where to go—
We follow the Holy Ghost
Who shows us so
>>>>
Into the woods
Walking quietly
Night owl asking *who?*
Crickets talking too
Energy knows
Where to go—
We follow the Holy Ghost
Who shows us so
>>>>
Fire inside
Leads us to look for
Ideals we lean toward
Ideas radical
Energy knows
Where to go—
We follow the Holy Ghost
Who shows us so
>>>>
Into the smoke
Asking allies
Join us creating
This inspired life
Energy knows
Where to go—
We follow the Holy Ghost
Who shows us so

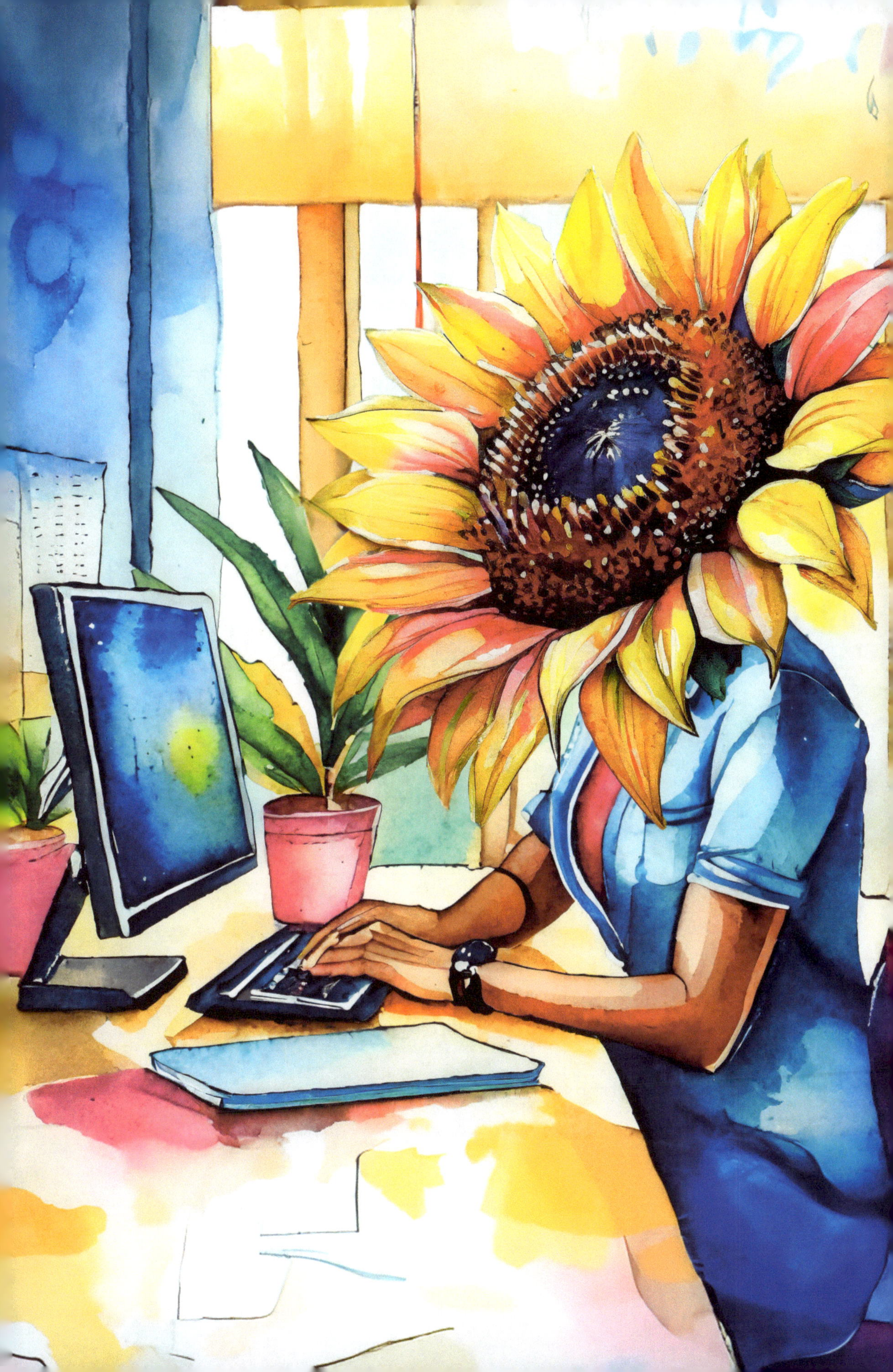

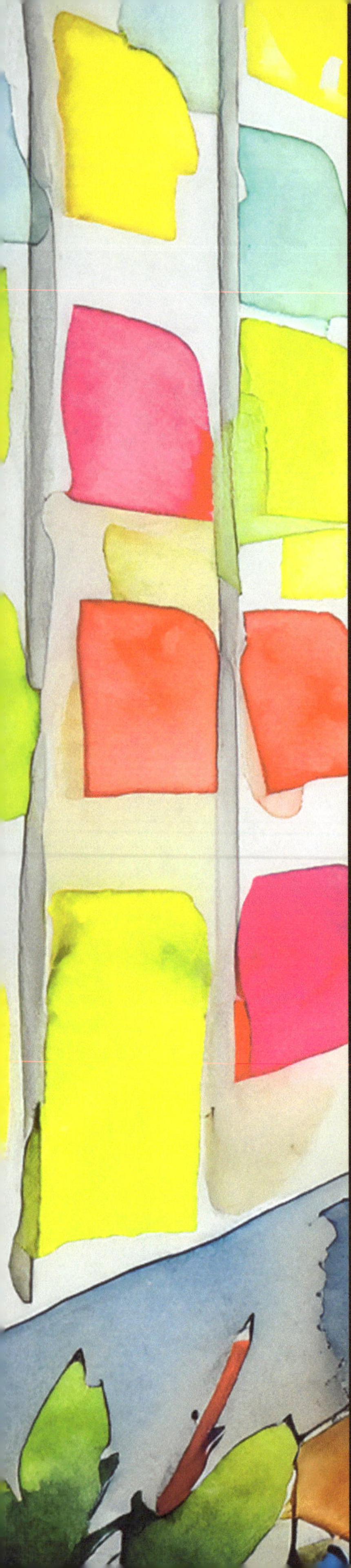

SUN DAY

Yesterday was a Sun day
Tomorrow is a Sun day
And today like yesterday
Is a Sun day
Last weekend
I was thinking
"Where is the Sun I'm seeking?"
Right after I defined it
I left the house to find it
Yesterday was a Sun day...
Last winds day
I was listening
To the breezes whispering
They told me
"Do not look down—
Sun is all around you"
Yesterday was a Sun day...
Last moon day was a rain day
It was a plain day
It was a gloomy day
But I found the Sun today
Today is a Sun day
Yesterday was a Sun day...
Today is a Sun day
My vibe is radiating
Today is an awesome day
Today is amazing

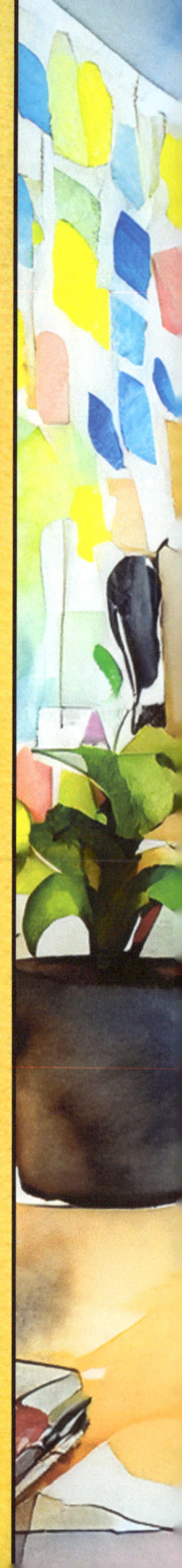

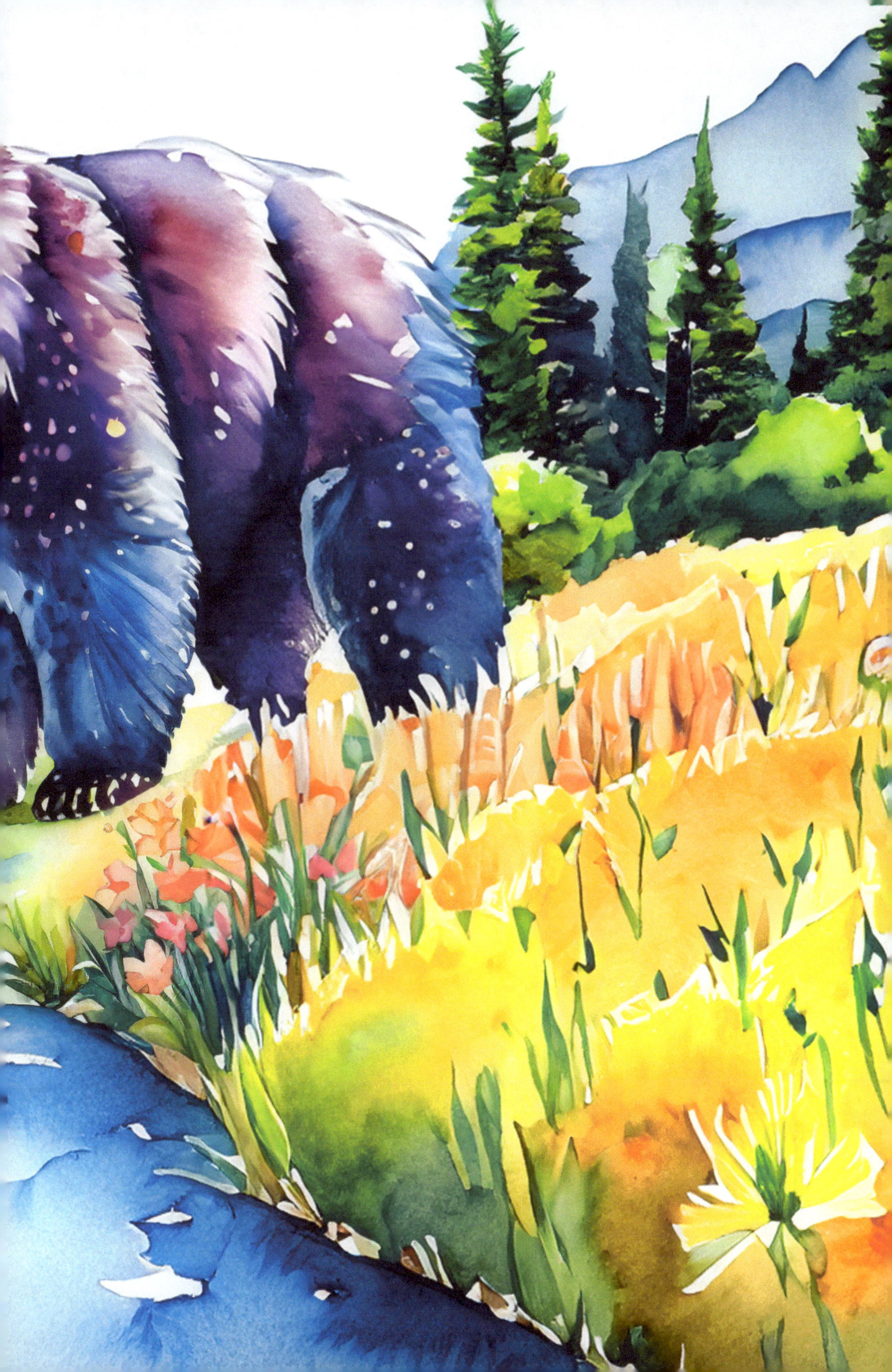

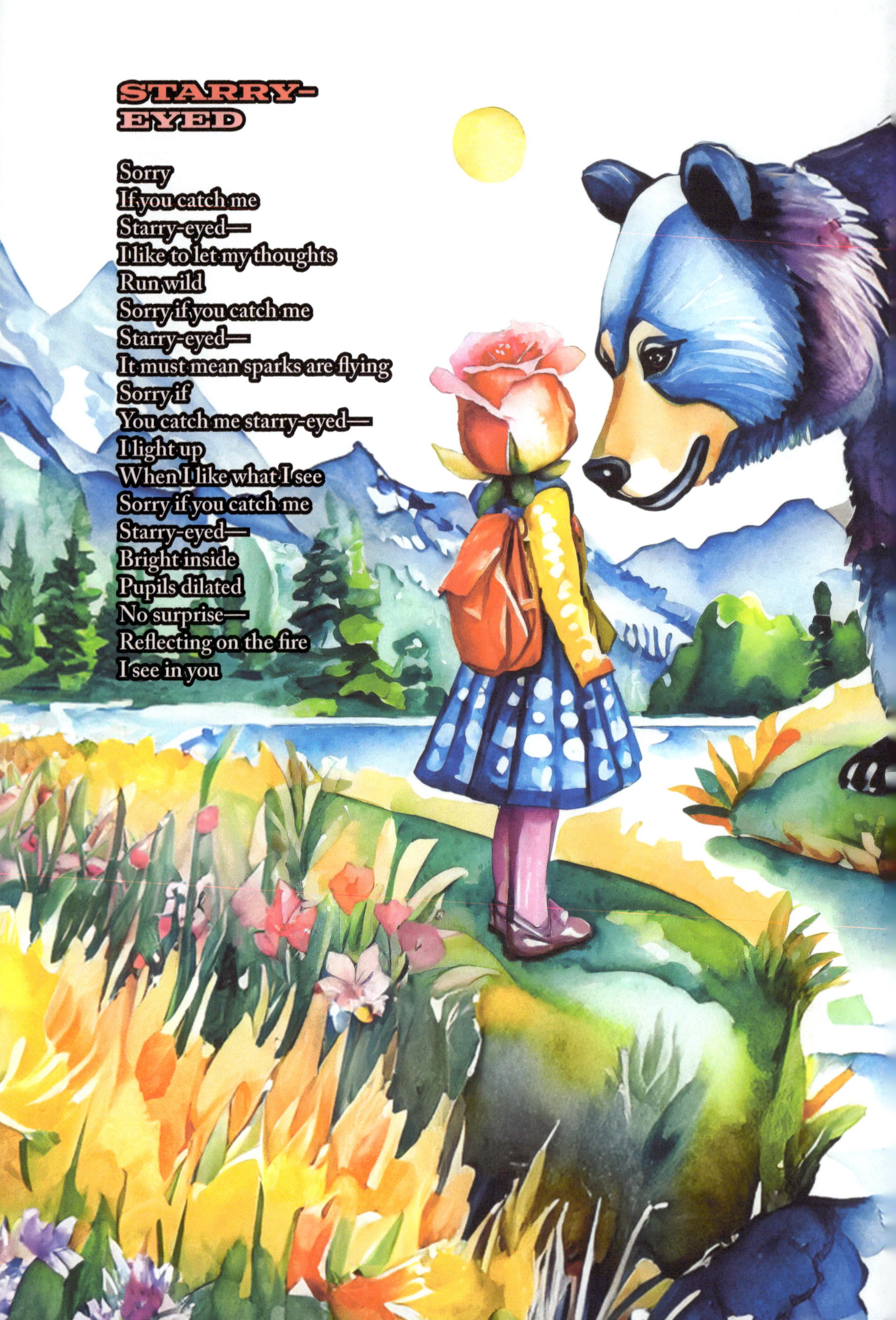

STARRY-
EYED

Sorry
If you catch me
Starry-eyed—
I like to let my thoughts
Run wild
Sorry if you catch me
Starry-eyed—
It must mean sparks are flying
Sorry if
You catch me starry-eyed—
I light up
When I like what I see
Sorry if you catch me
Starry-eyed—
Bright inside
Pupils dilated
No surprise—
Reflecting on the fire
I see in you

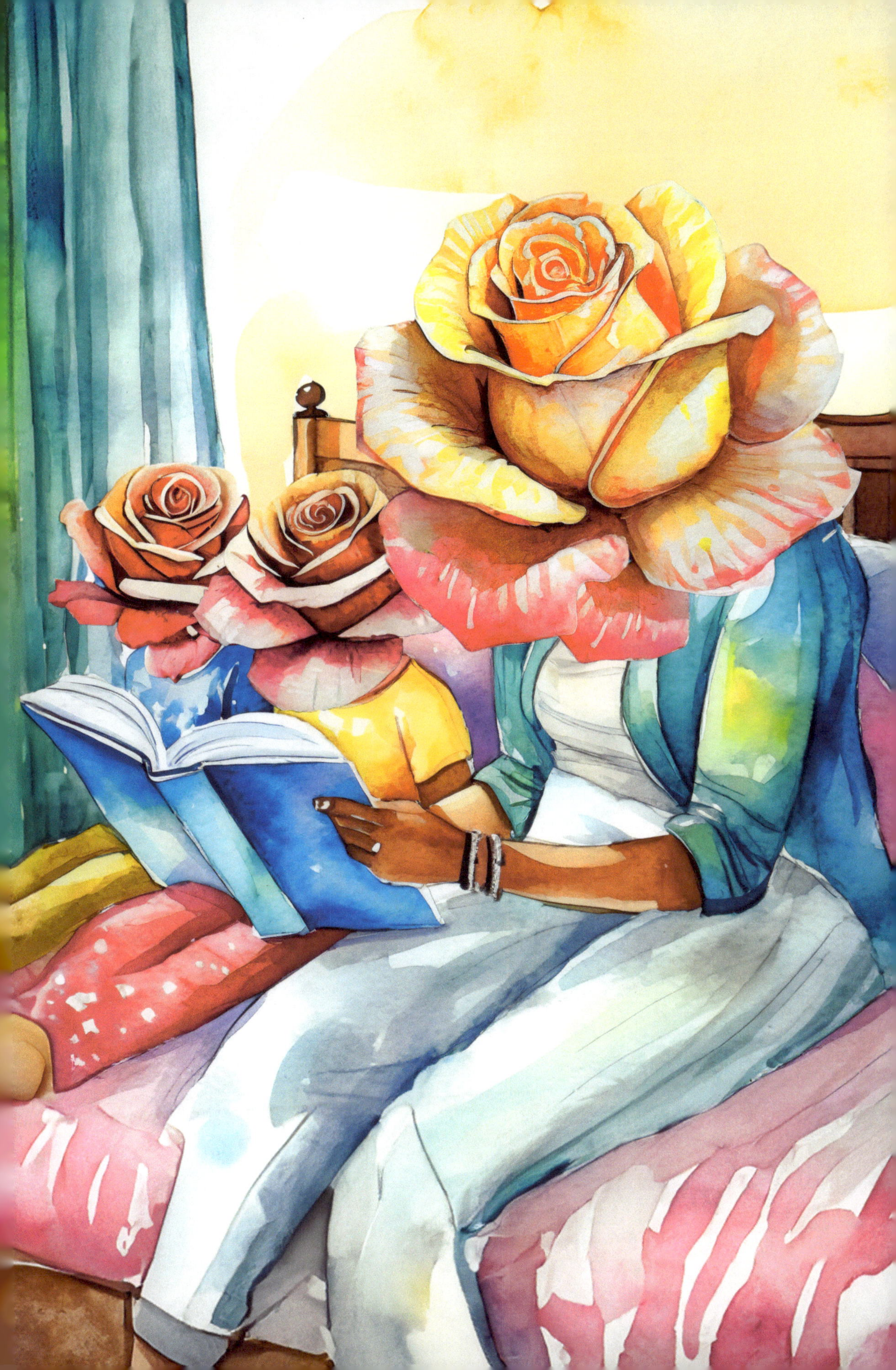

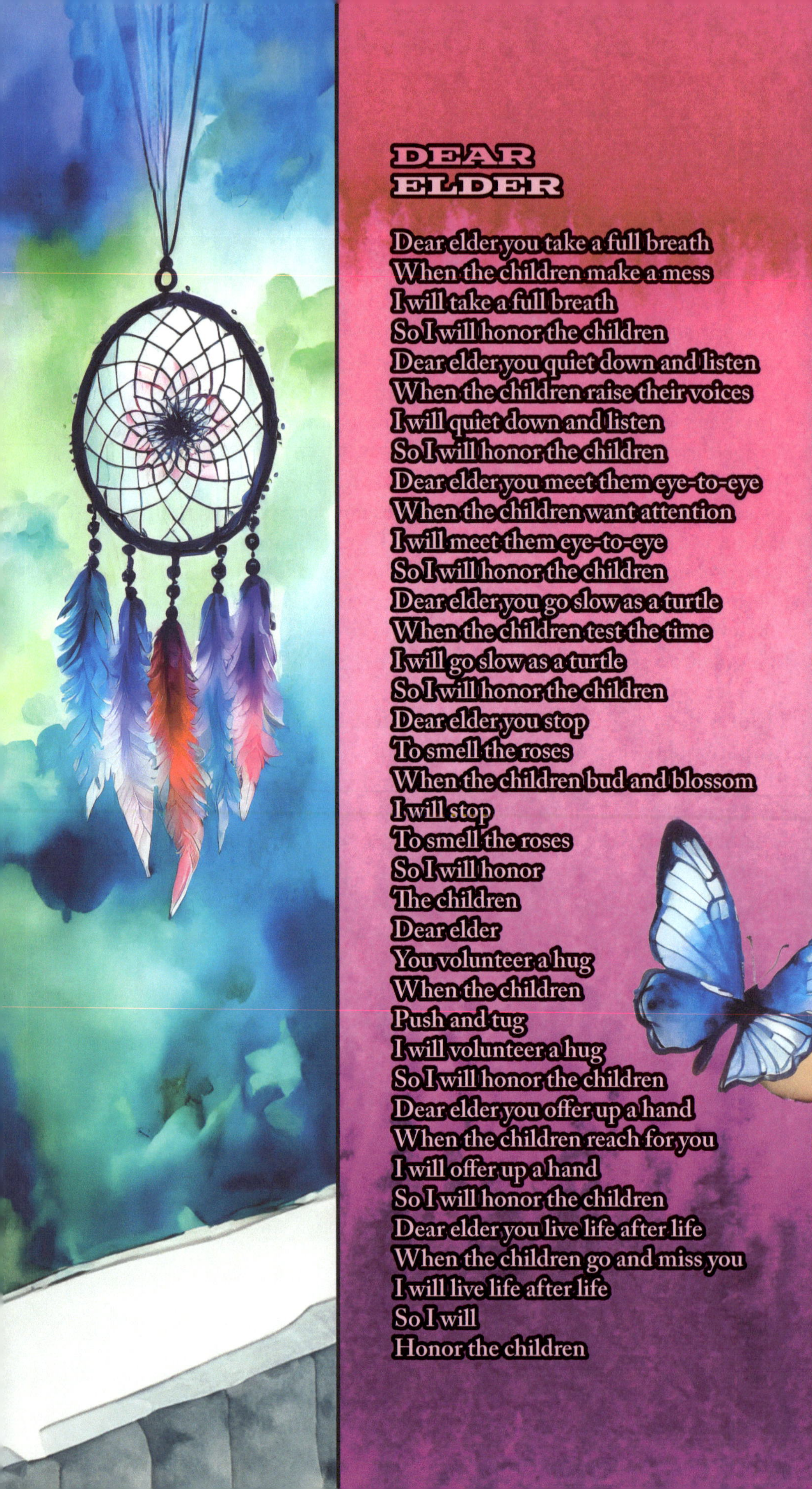

DEAR
ELDER

Dear elder, you take a full breath
When the children make a mess
I will take a full breath
So I will honor the children
Dear elder, you quiet down and listen
When the children raise their voices
I will quiet down and listen
So I will honor the children
Dear elder, you meet them eye-to-eye
When the children want attention
I will meet them eye-to-eye
So I will honor the children
Dear elder, you go slow as a turtle
When the children test the time
I will go slow as a turtle
So I will honor the children
Dear elder, you stop
To smell the roses
When the children bud and blossom
I will stop
To smell the roses
So I will honor
The children
Dear elder
You volunteer a hug
When the children
Push and tug
I will volunteer a hug
So I will honor the children
Dear elder, you offer up a hand
When the children reach for you
I will offer up a hand
So I will honor the children
Dear elder, you live life after life
When the children go and miss you
I will live life after life
So I will
Honor the children

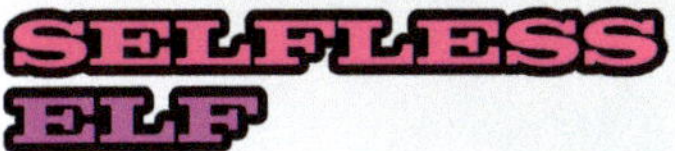

SELFLESS ELF

Your brother becomes
Someone else—
A selfless elf
Someone smaller
A no-name gnome
Unknown but not alone
Unnoticed yet never needy
An ego dissolves
As egos go
As a rosebush grows
Thorns and petals
As a rosebud blooms
I bloom too—
Into a bedtime song carrier
Book reader writer
Provider
Tickle monster
Authority figure
Always never sometimes
Your brother faces
A daughter in a diaper
A son in a fit
A mother in surrender
A man in a mirror
Facing rage
Powerless to the powers
Of other flowers
Humiliation
Limitation
Trapped—
An eagle in a birdcage
A buffalo frozen in snow
A caterpillar in a cocoon
Wishing to butterfly out

LOVE IS TRUE

In a time of insecurity
Facing fears of betrayal
I ask God for faith
In the universe
Then I catch myself—
Asking to believe
In something nonexistent
When everything anything
Nonexistent
Does not deserve my faith
I remember now—
The universe does not exist
But there is hope
Because I know
Love is true
>>>>
Even in insecurity
While I question what exists
I see through the clutter—
Love does not waver
This is how I know
Love is real
Even when all else is lost
Wavering spiraling
Even facing abandonment—
Again again again
The disappearance of the universe
Does not affect the fact
That Love is Truth
This is the ultimate truth
It sets me free

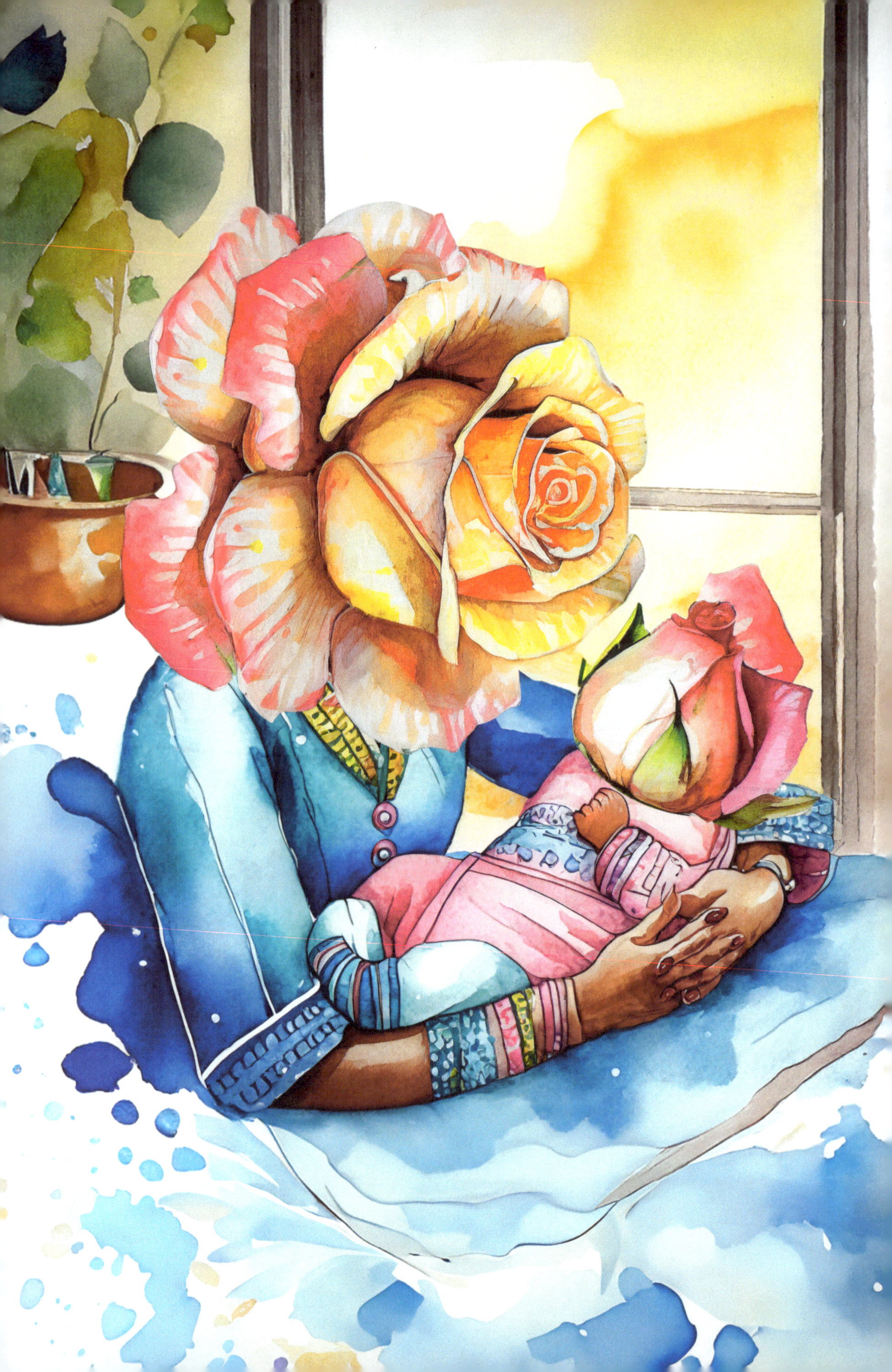

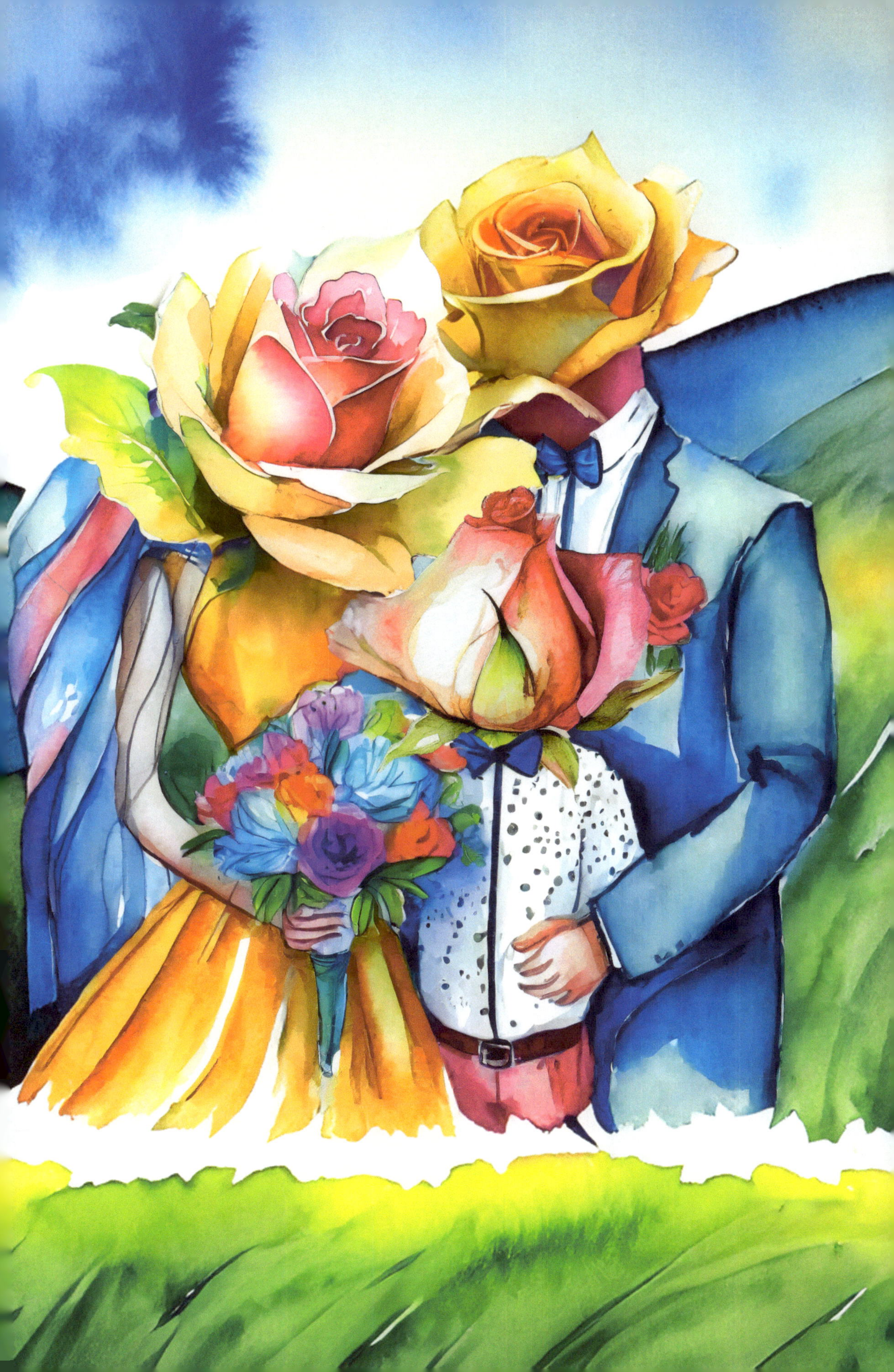

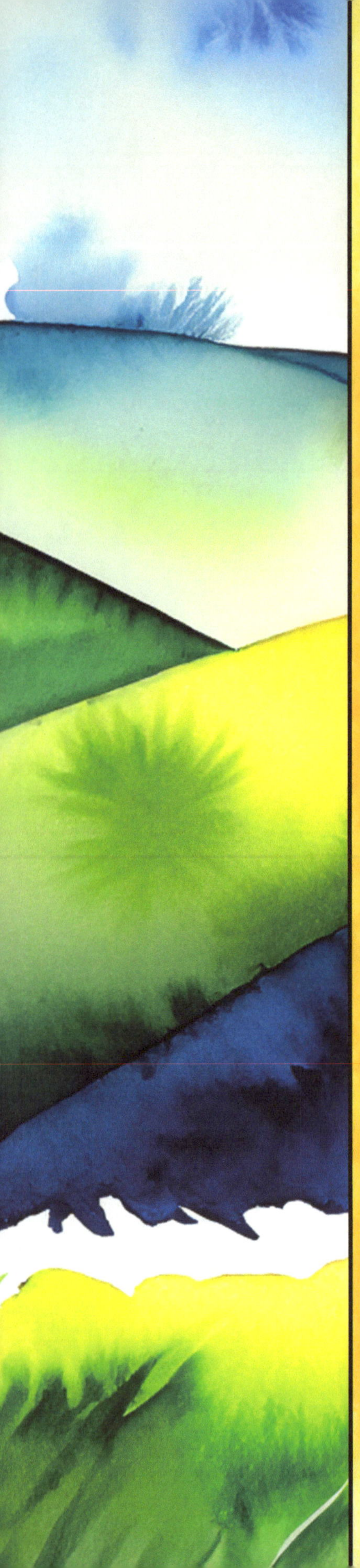

RINGS TRUE

Your brother
Stands on a hilltop
In a flashy suit
Beside a golden bride
Inviting seven generations
And the four directions
To encircle us
In infinite love
So it is—
Even as the ring bearer
Loses the wedding rings
In the flower field—
Everyone searching
Until the rings find their way
To waiting fingers
Even as a child
Wanders up the hill
Curious as 2-year-olds are
"Who is this man
Who stands by my mama?"
Wondering
"Where do I stand?"
Interrupting the ceremony—
Attention shifts
From a serious speech
To a silly smile
As the child bounces
In his daddy's loving arms
While his rad daddy
Rests in the loving arms
Of the wind the Sun
The water the earth
Above below
The Innermost
> > > >
In this way
Your brother becomes
A family man

44 DOORS

Through 44 doors
33 homes by age 22
11 years a young adult
Zero inner child
My soul willingly crosses
Worldly thresholds
Obsessed with overachievement
Possessed by self-importance
Distressed by impatience
Worrying my way
Through pain points
Carrying the weight of the wait
Racing toward the future
Wanting what's next
Wishing to escape the past
Hurrying through
Hurt feelings burdens
Wondering where I belong
When I am lost
In the ego trip of ego trips
Hiding my face
Behind a facade
Good from far but far from good
With all the time in all the times
With all the world of worlds
In 44 doors of 4getfulness
The truest part of me
4gets who I truly am—
4rever a soul

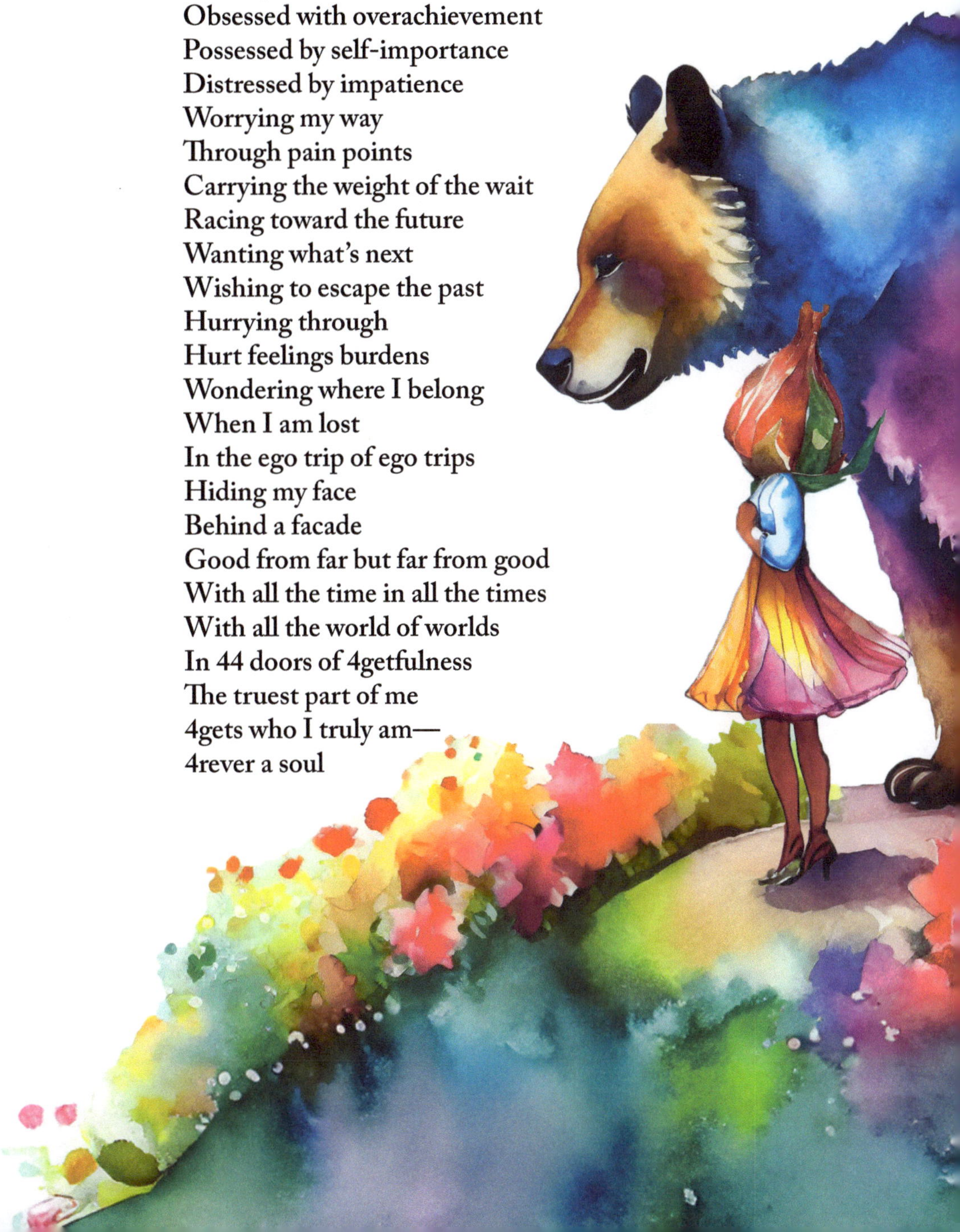

Those great outdoors
Through all their doors
Remain great
In all the ways—
Stony stairways petal pathways
Wet waterways arid roadways
Even those open portals
That go where no one knows
Nature knows its nature

In a valley of winds
Flowers sway on their stems
Opening blooms to the sunlight
Inviting bees and butterflies
To continue their dances
On dancing flower dance floors
In there enclosed in petal walls
A flower world moves and grooves
To music made by DJ Nature

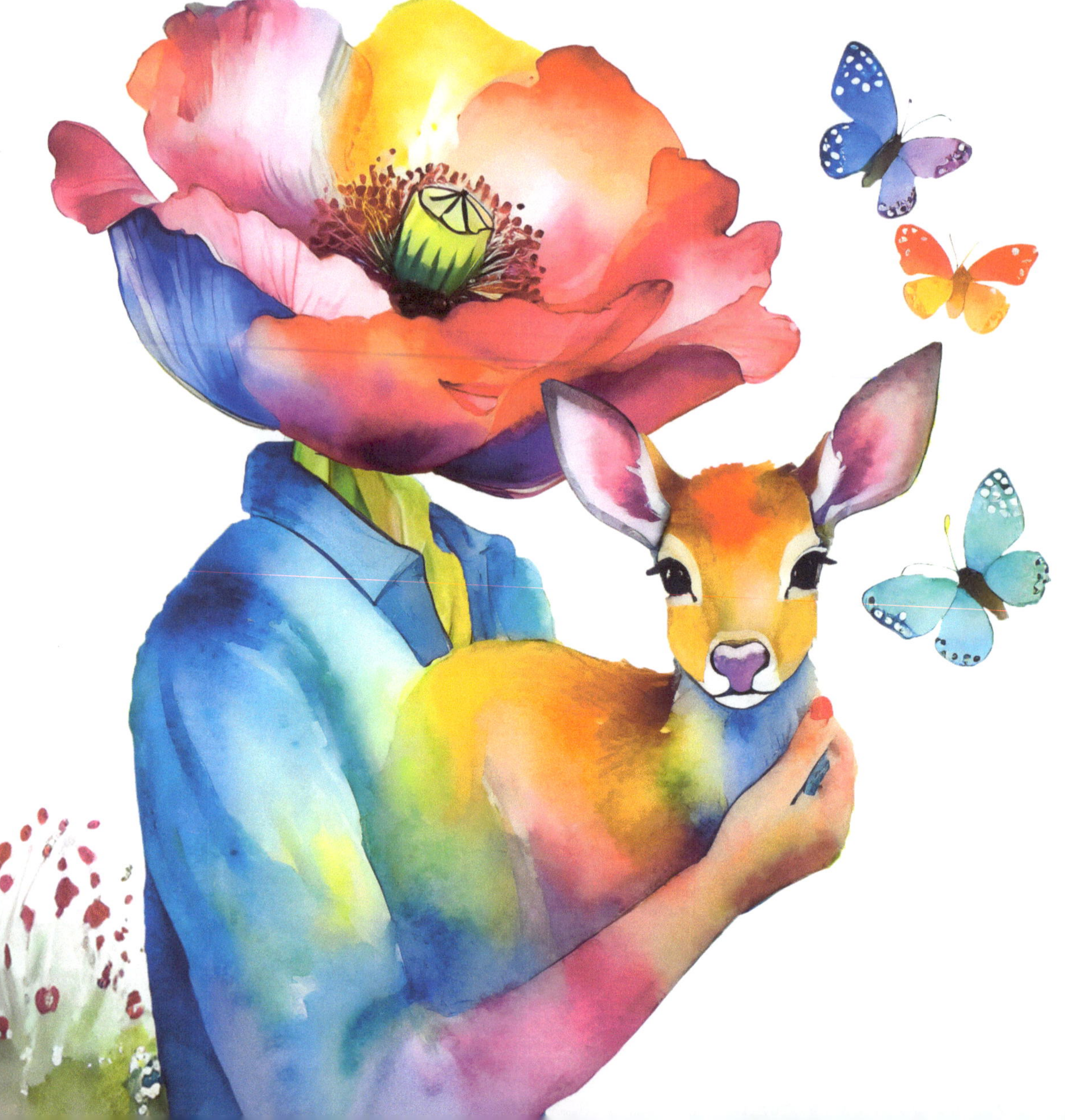

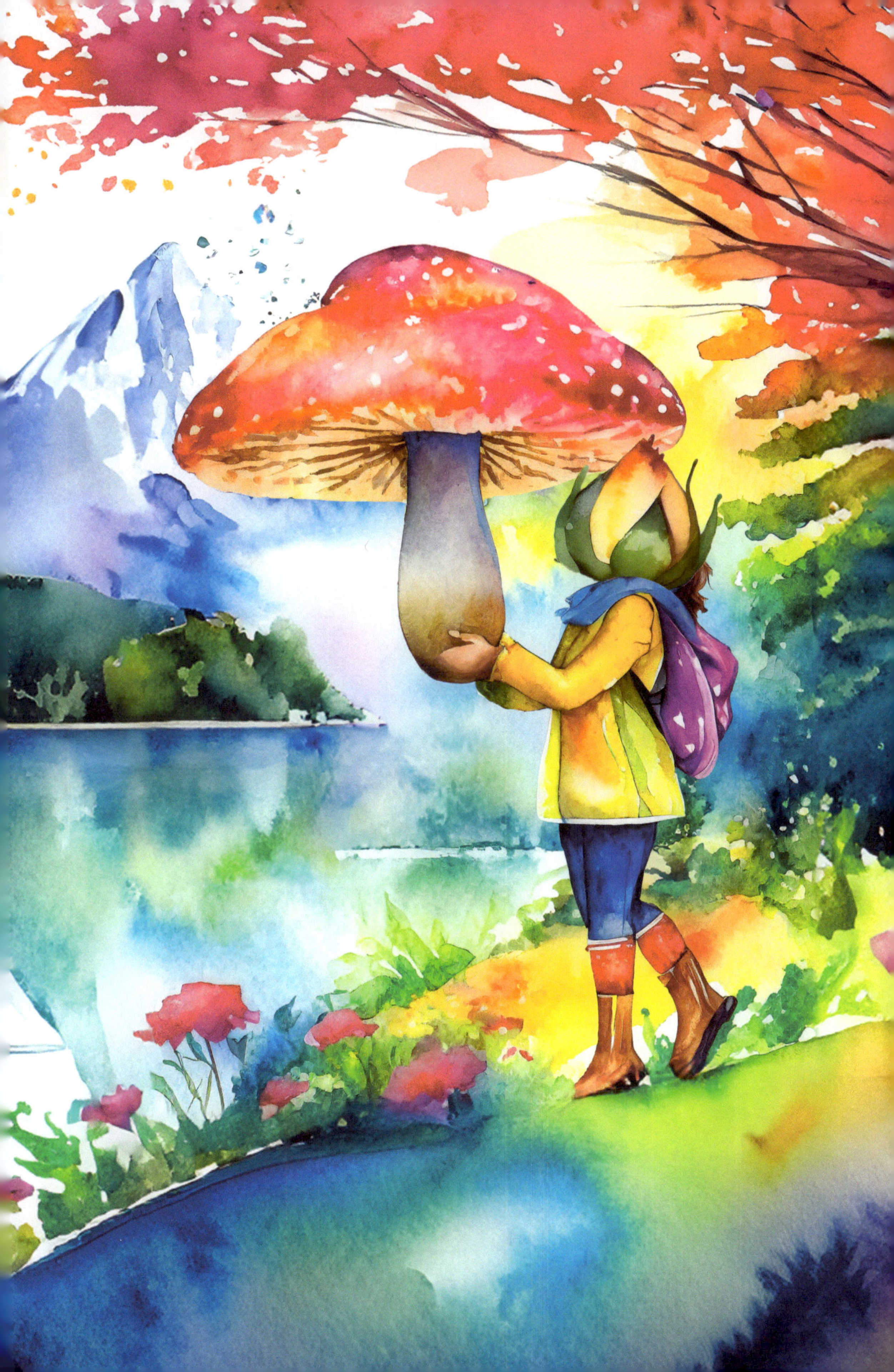

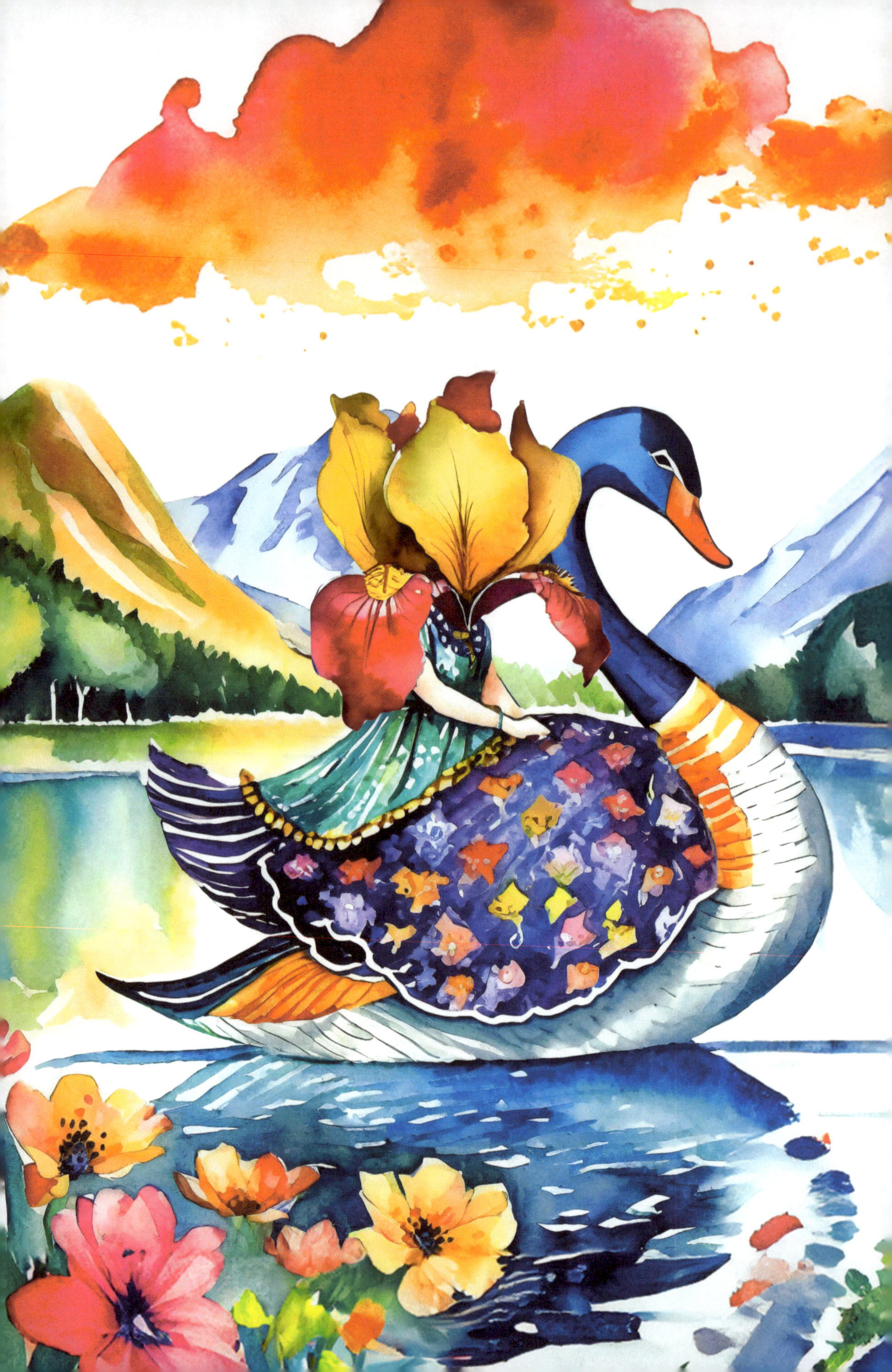

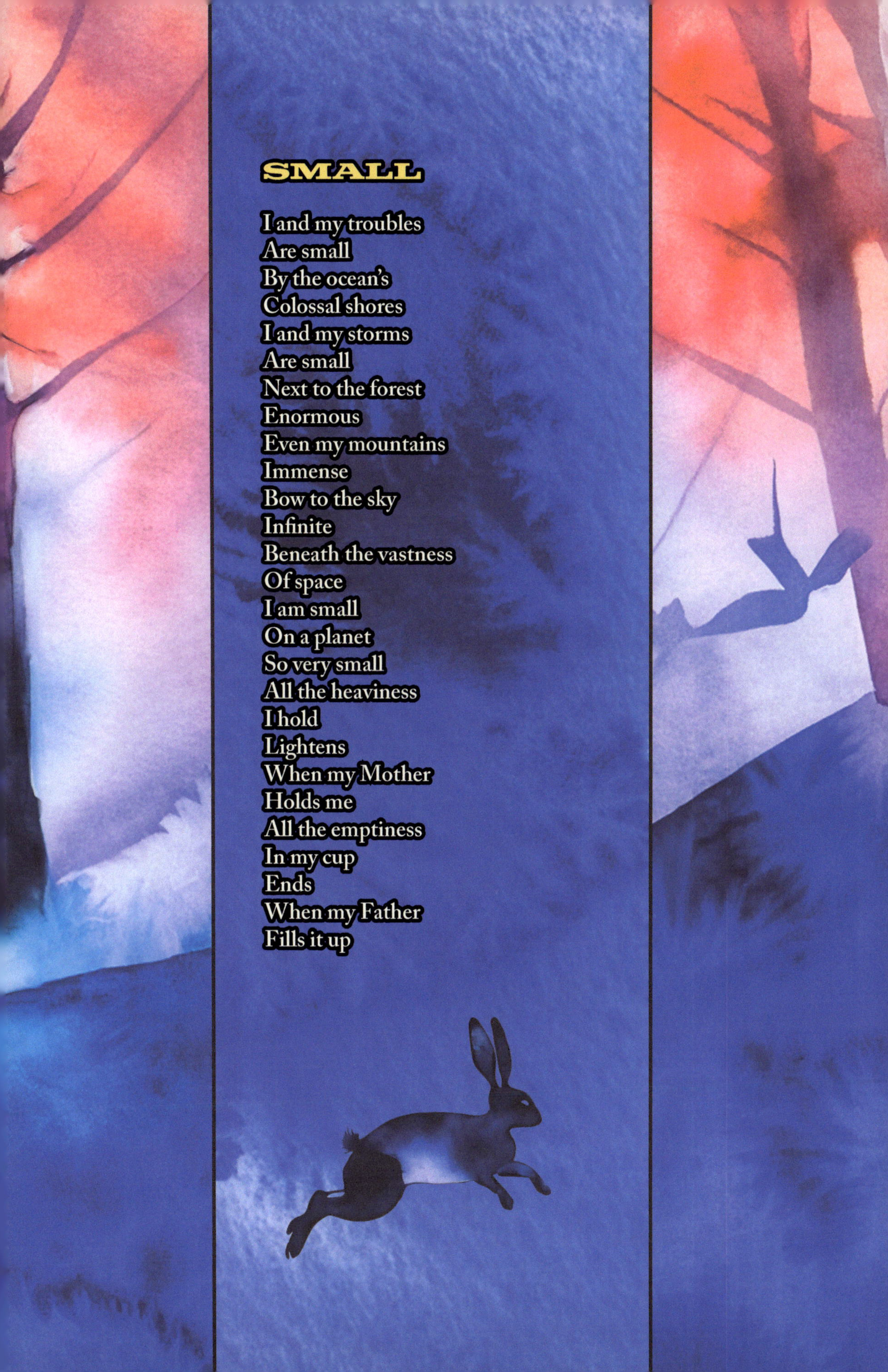

SMALL

I and my troubles
Are small
By the ocean's
Colossal shores
I and my storms
Are small
Next to the forest
Enormous
Even my mountains
Immense
Bow to the sky
Infinite
Beneath the vastness
Of space
I am small
On a planet
So very small
All the heaviness
I hold
Lightens
When my Mother
Holds me
All the emptiness
In my cup
Ends
When my Father
Fills it up

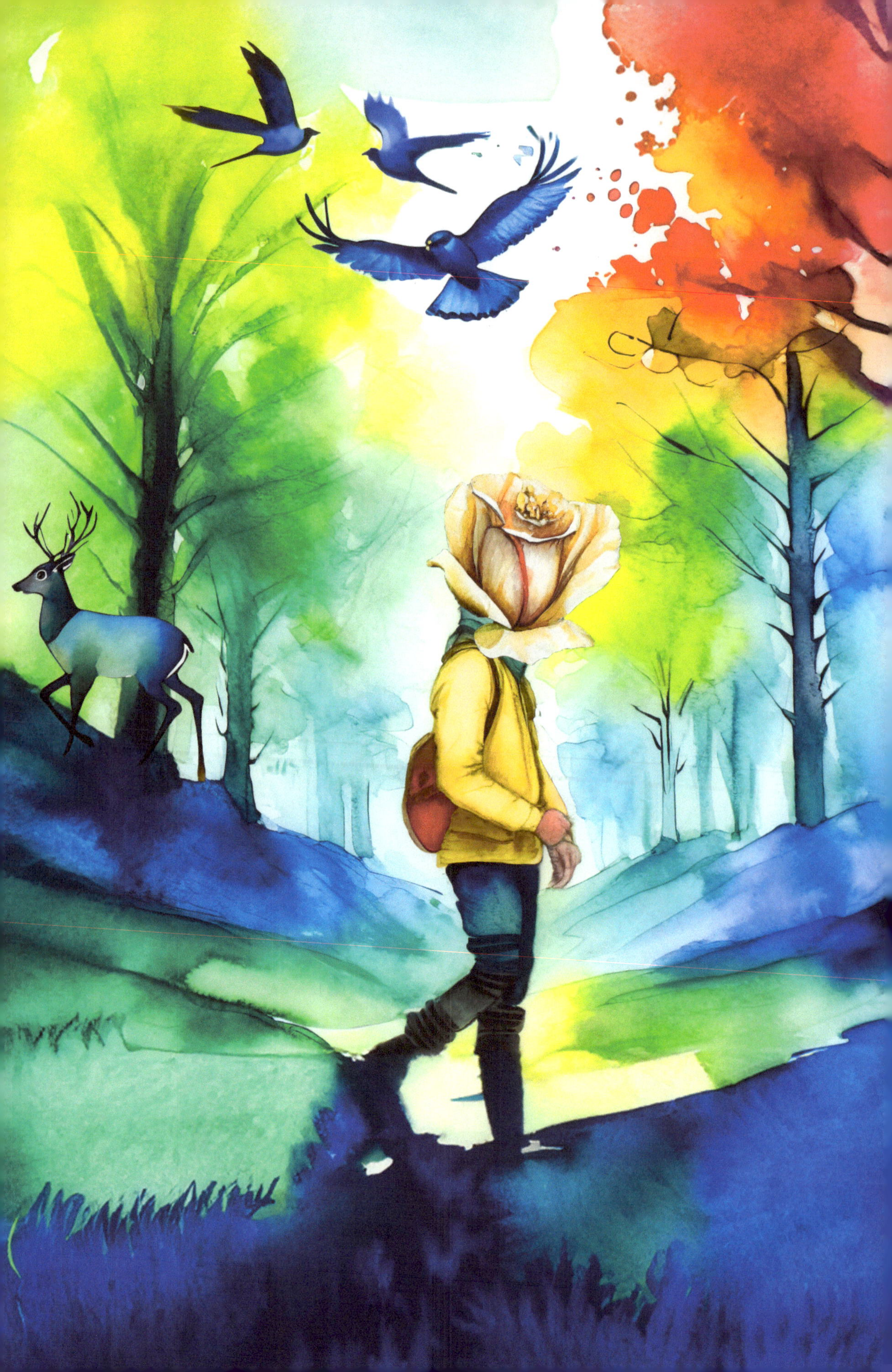

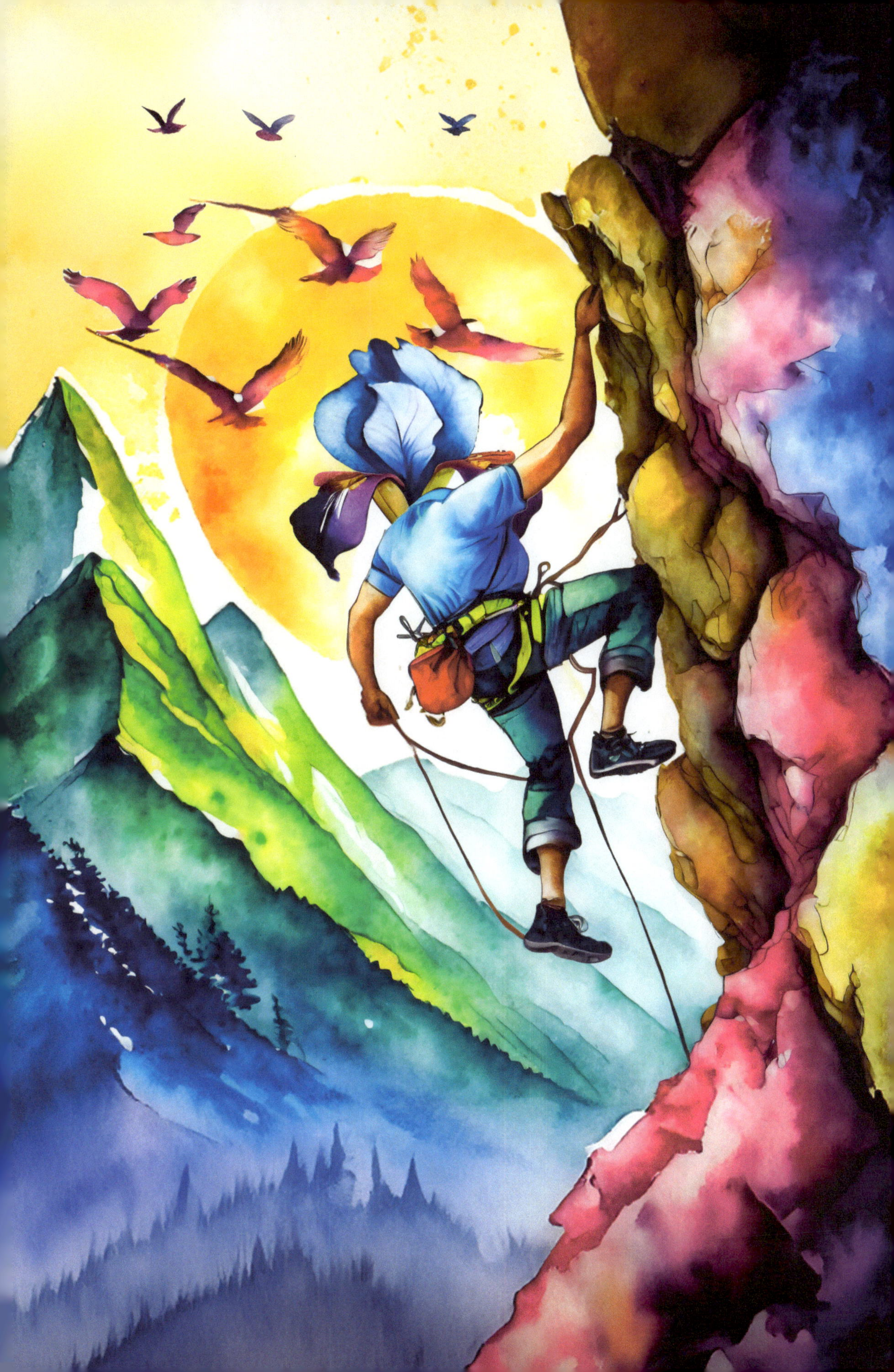

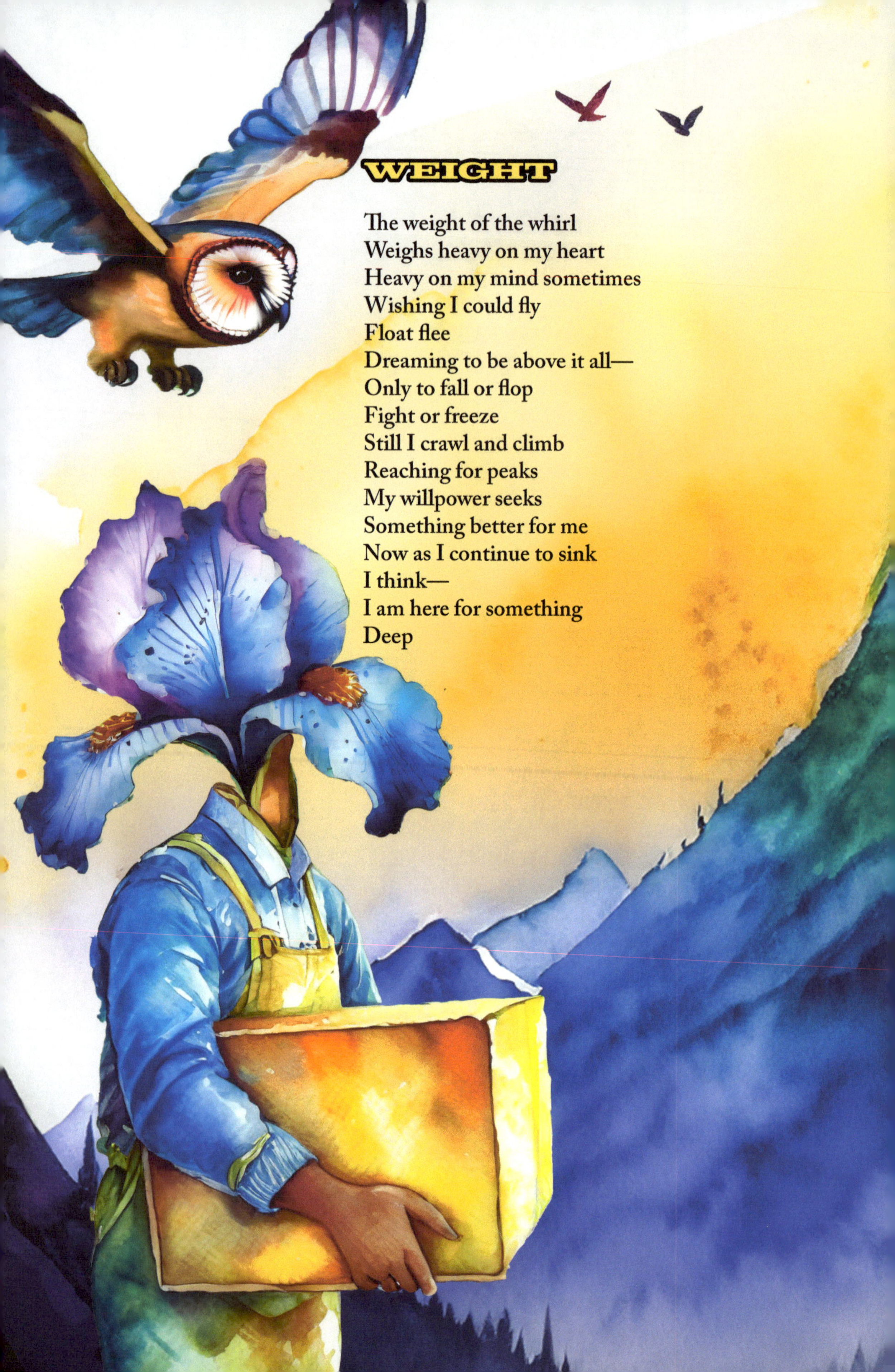

WEIGHT

The weight of the whirl
Weighs heavy on my heart
Heavy on my mind sometimes
Wishing I could fly
Float flee
Dreaming to be above it all—
Only to fall or flop
Fight or freeze
Still I crawl and climb
Reaching for peaks
My willpower seeks
Something better for me
Now as I continue to sink
I think—
I am here for something
Deep

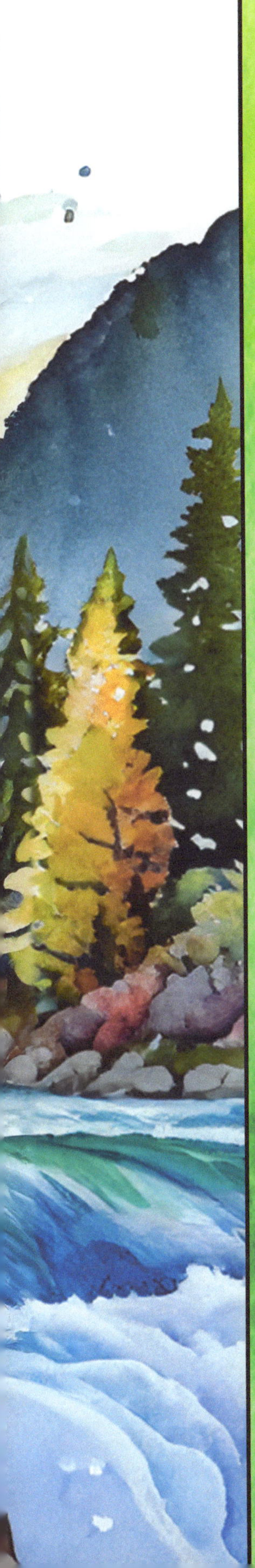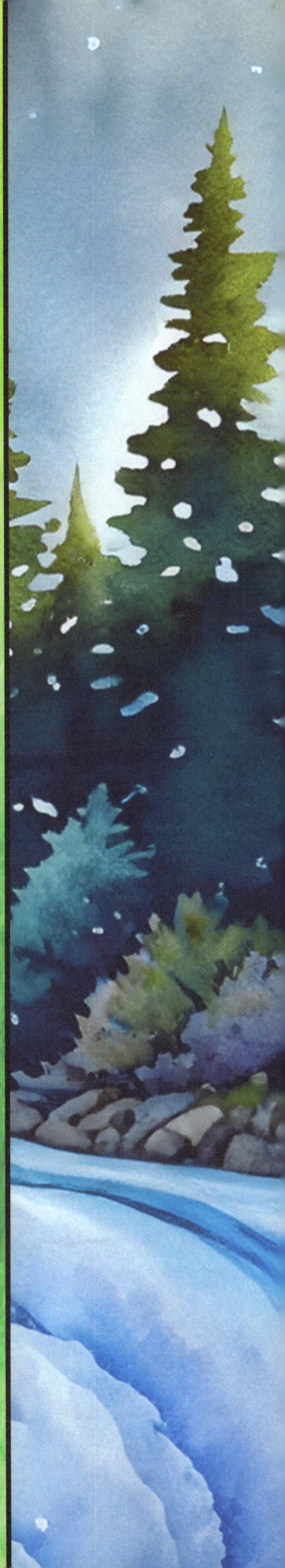

DROPS BY ONE

How can I forget
Those mountain towns
Where elevation
Exceeds population
Where everyone feels the loss
When the population drops
By one
I wonder
If fishermen wonder—
Where are the fish?
What are they eating?
There's no one to ask
When they go alone to fishing holes
I wonder if they wonder—
Where are the bears?
Are we alone?
I wonder if anyone wonders
Why a whitewater river
Spins and sinks
Out of sight
Whirlpooling
To untold depths
I wonder why
The whirlpool of whirlpools here
Swallows this river now
As a fisherman falls in
Never seen again
The population drops by one
Everyone feels the loss—
I wonder
If fishermen wonder—
Where does the portal go?
I wonder—
Who am I without my dad?
Less of a son
More of a man
All of a sudden

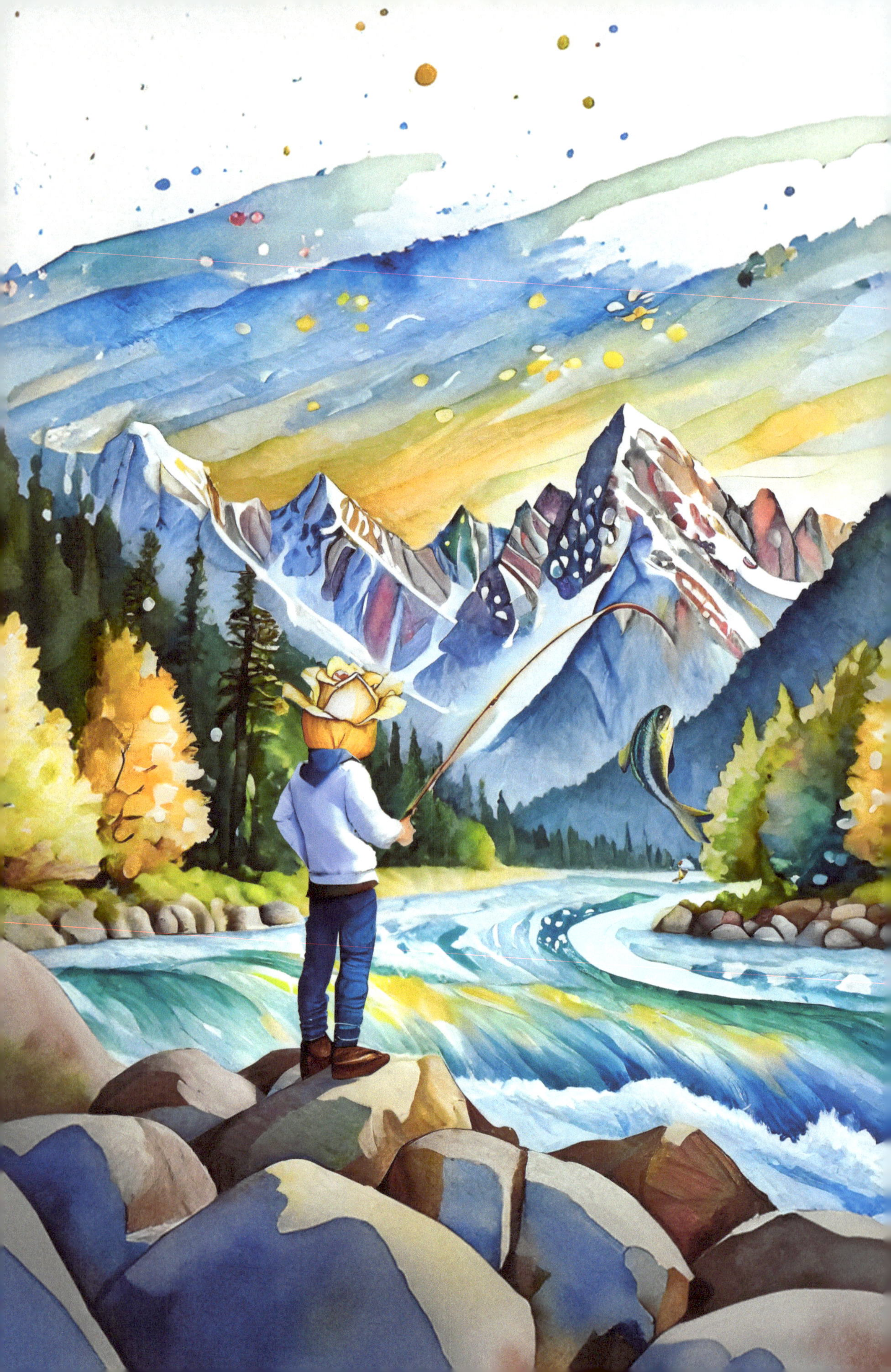

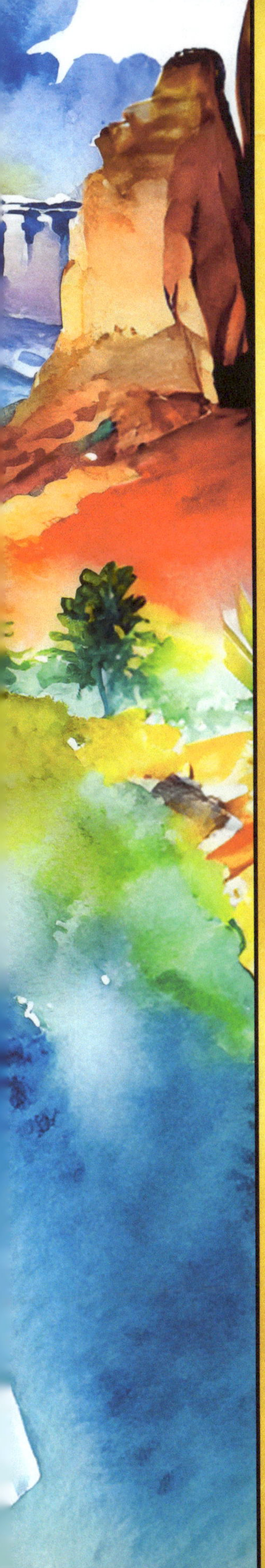

WAKE
UP
CALLS

We awaken
To meadowlark songs
As dawn breaks
Maracas shake in rattlesnakes
As we roam rugged roads
The air whispers
Through us
Like reeds
Like cottonwood trees
We go Home
When the Sun rises
Fiery bright
High desert life seeks shade
Congregating in stony caves
Hiding in holes
> > > >
Ooh an owl speaks
From a juniper tree—
Who? Who?
Who are we?
Wildflowers wildfires
Wildlife
Always never sometimes
We burn we sting we bring relief
Comfort comes
When rainclouds guide us Home
Raindrops arrive with rainbows
Sagebrush fragrance wafts
In the prairie winds
Antelope dash across cacti
Jackrabbits run under rabbitbrush
They lead our minds
To ancient times
When everyone is with us
In a spacious place
Where everywhere is faraway
Only in our hearts
Everwild we are—
Always never sometimes
Home

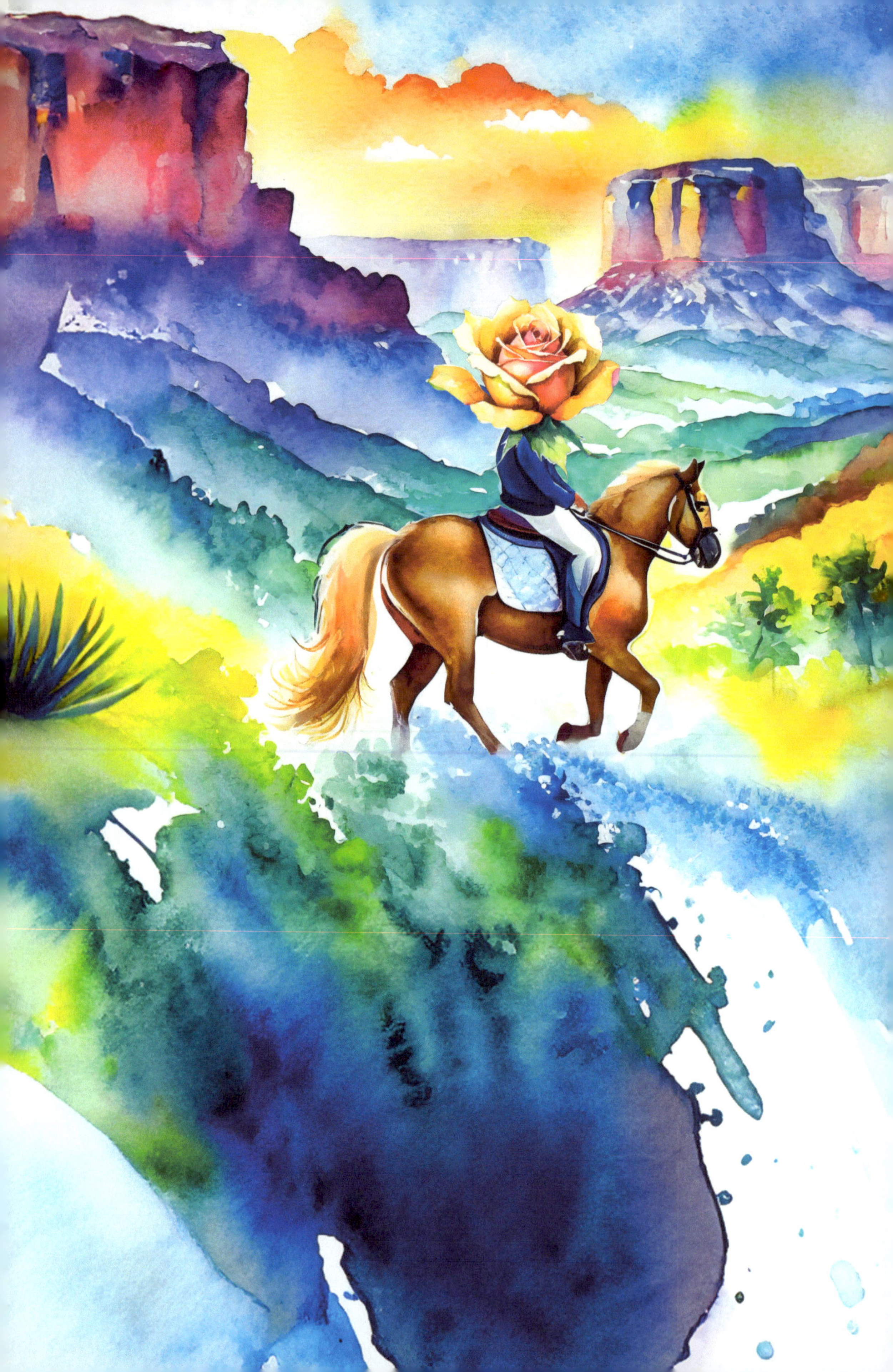

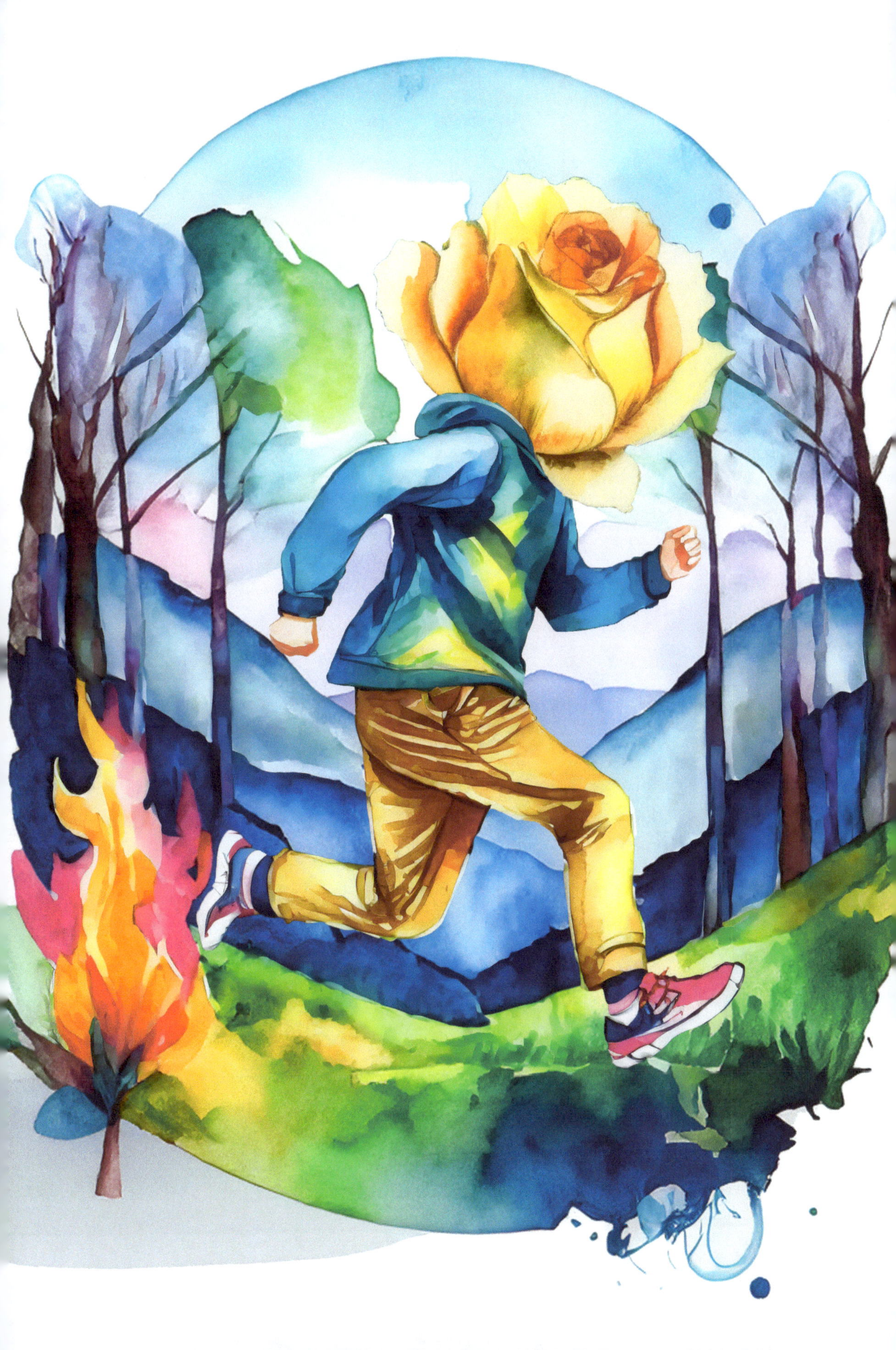

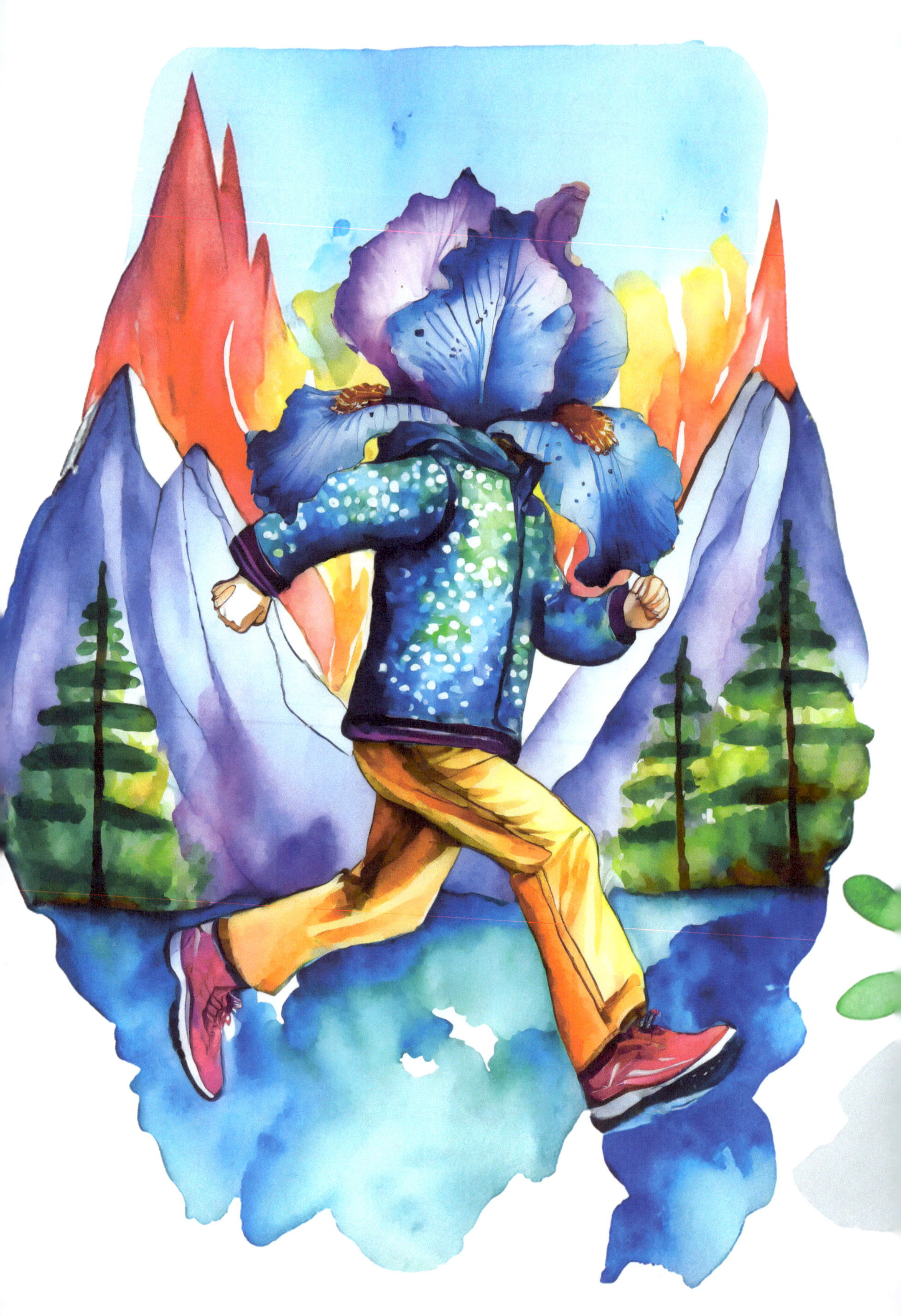

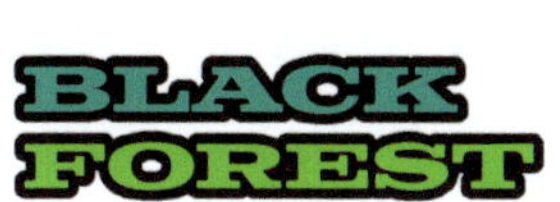

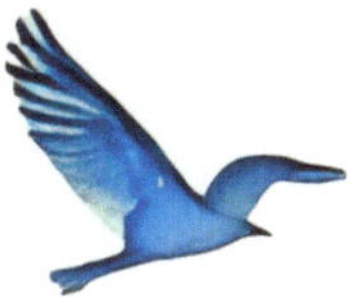

BLACK FOREST

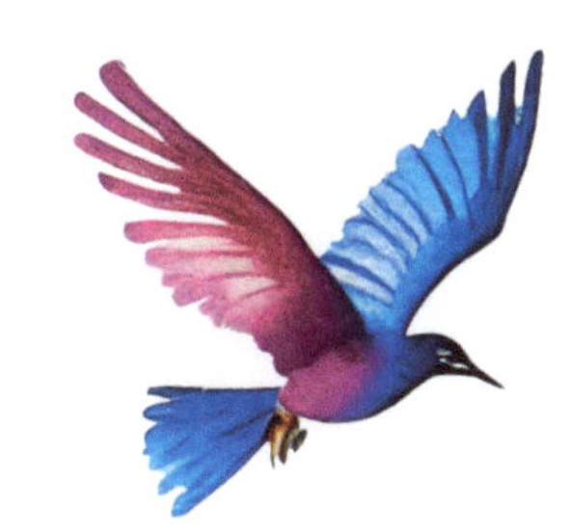

A black forest
Grows evergreen again
And this boy fires forward
Full blast blessed blissful—
Like a rock in God's slingshot

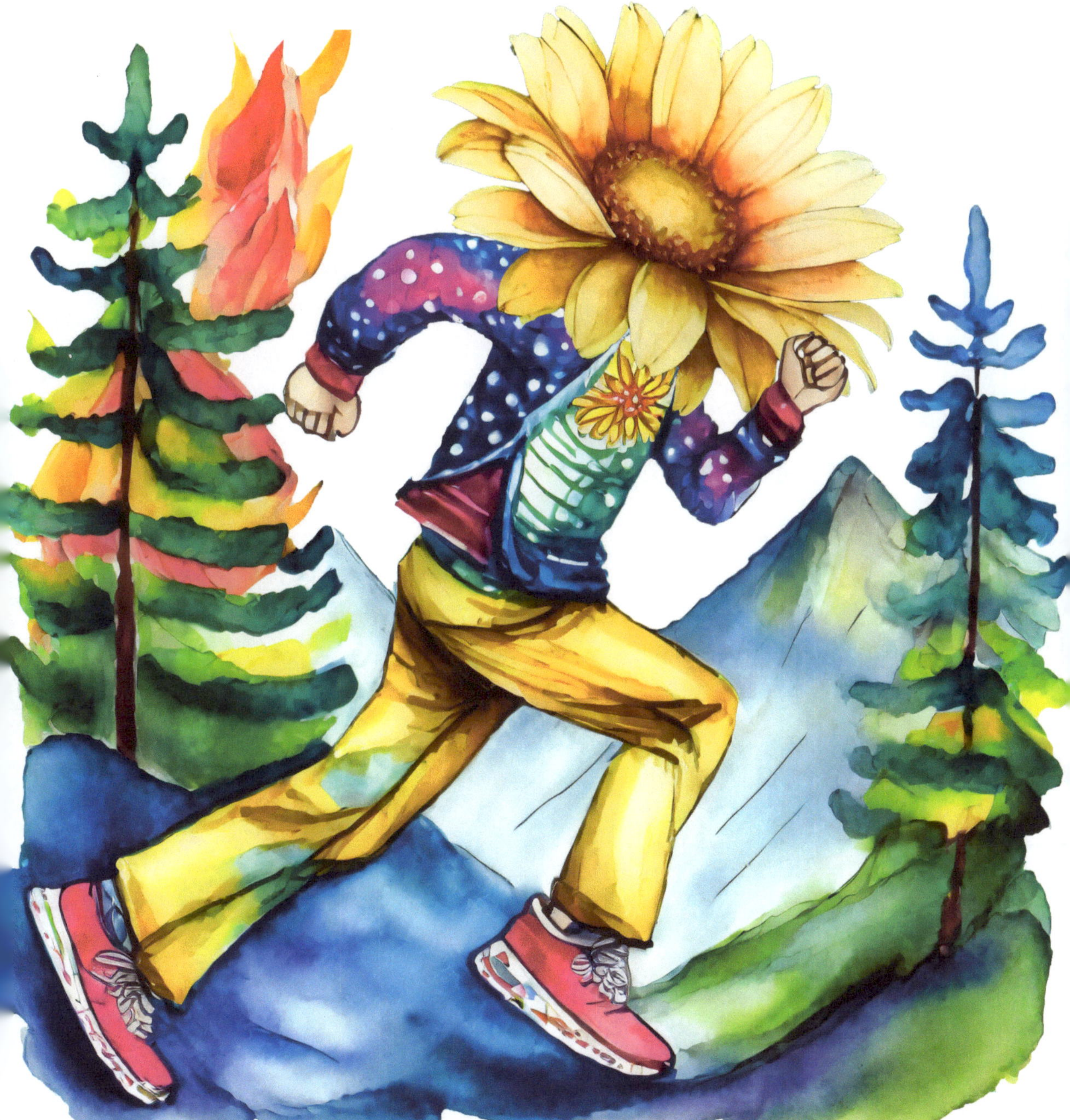

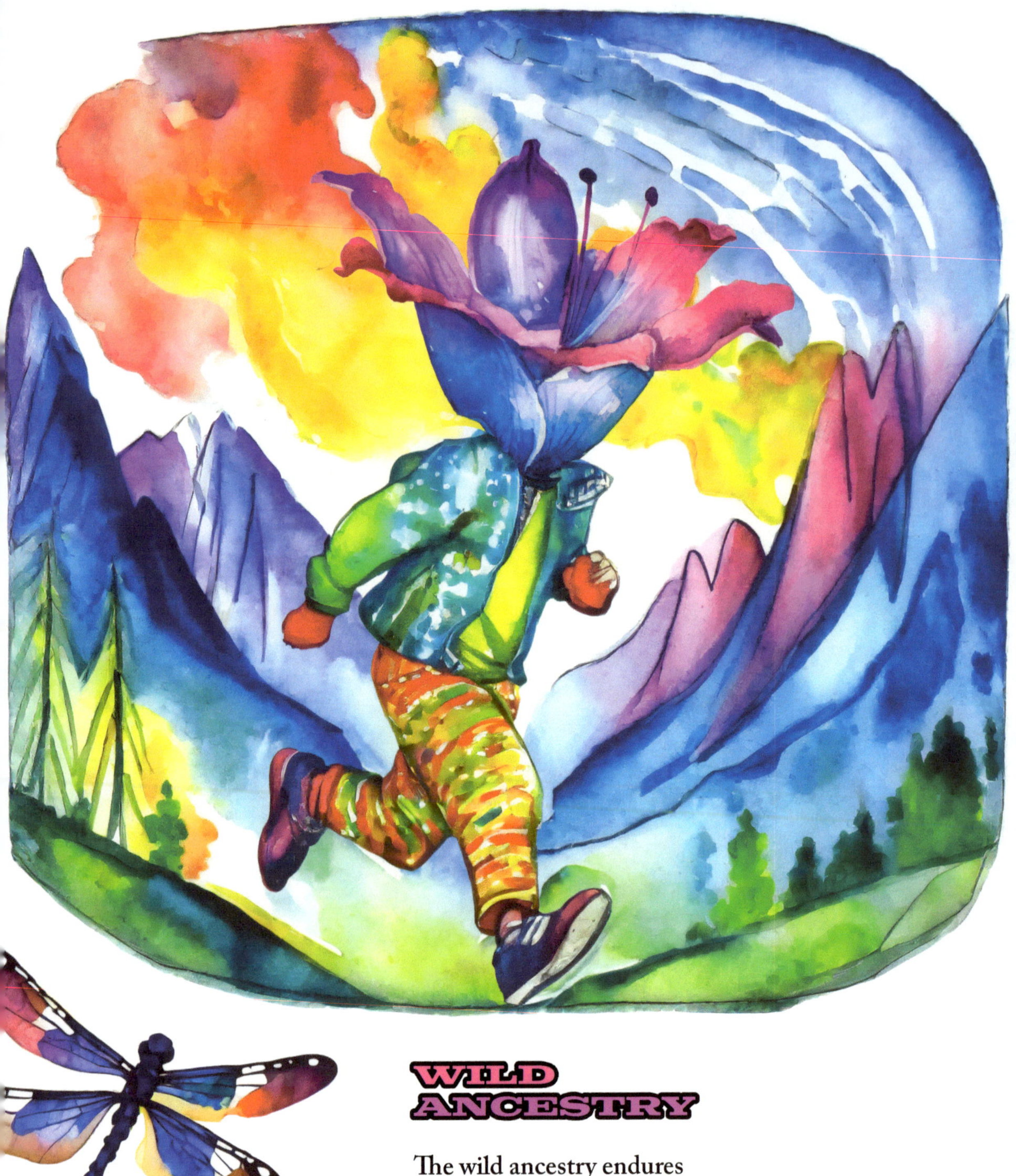

WILD ANCESTRY

The wild ancestry endures
In Yellowstone
Where buffalo roam
Western meadowlarks sing
Indian paintbrushes
Paint the fields red orange yellow
Even after wildfires
Silence the wildlife
For a while

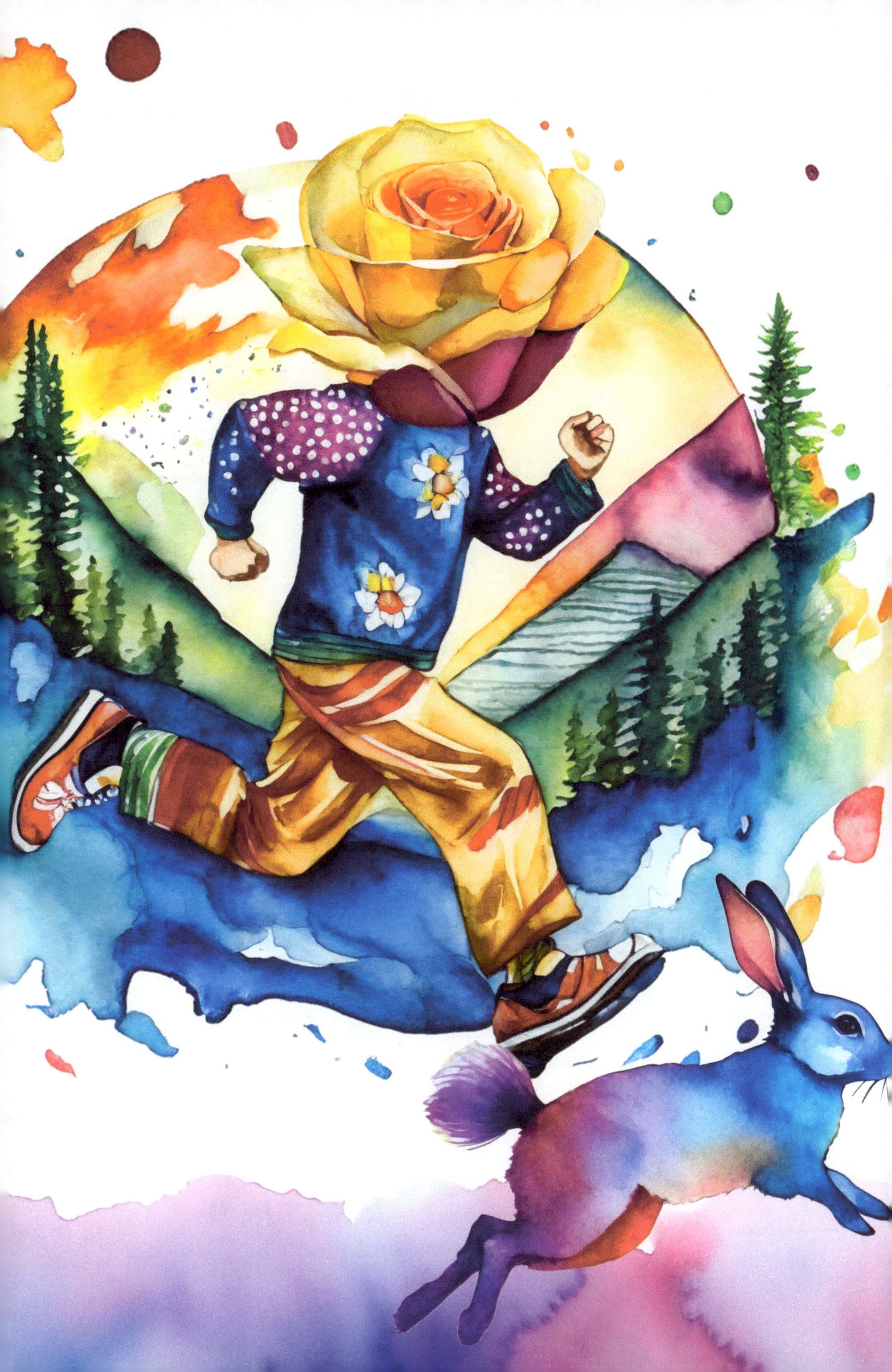

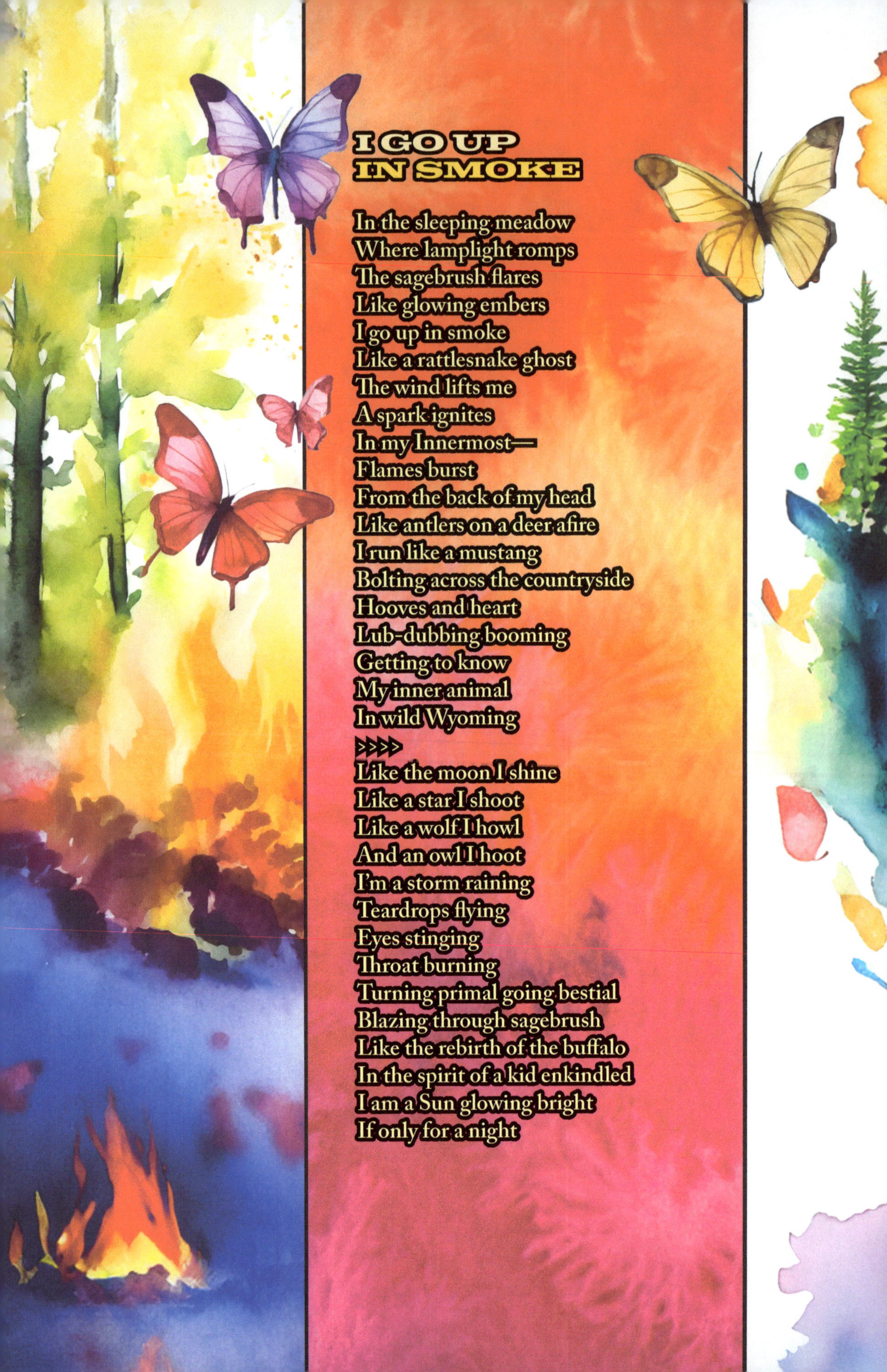

I GO UP
IN SMOKE

In the sleeping meadow
Where lamplight romps
The sagebrush flares
Like glowing embers
I go up in smoke
Like a rattlesnake ghost
The wind lifts me
A spark ignites
In my Innermost—
Flames burst
From the back of my head
Like antlers on a deer afire
I run like a mustang
Bolting across the countryside
Hooves and heart
Lub-dubbing booming
Getting to know
My inner animal
In wild Wyoming
>>>>
Like the moon I shine
Like a star I shoot
Like a wolf I howl
And an owl I hoot
I'm a storm raining
Teardrops flying
Eyes stinging
Throat burning
Turning primal going bestial
Blazing through sagebrush
Like the rebirth of the buffalo
In the spirit of a kid enkindled
I am a Sun glowing bright
If only for a night

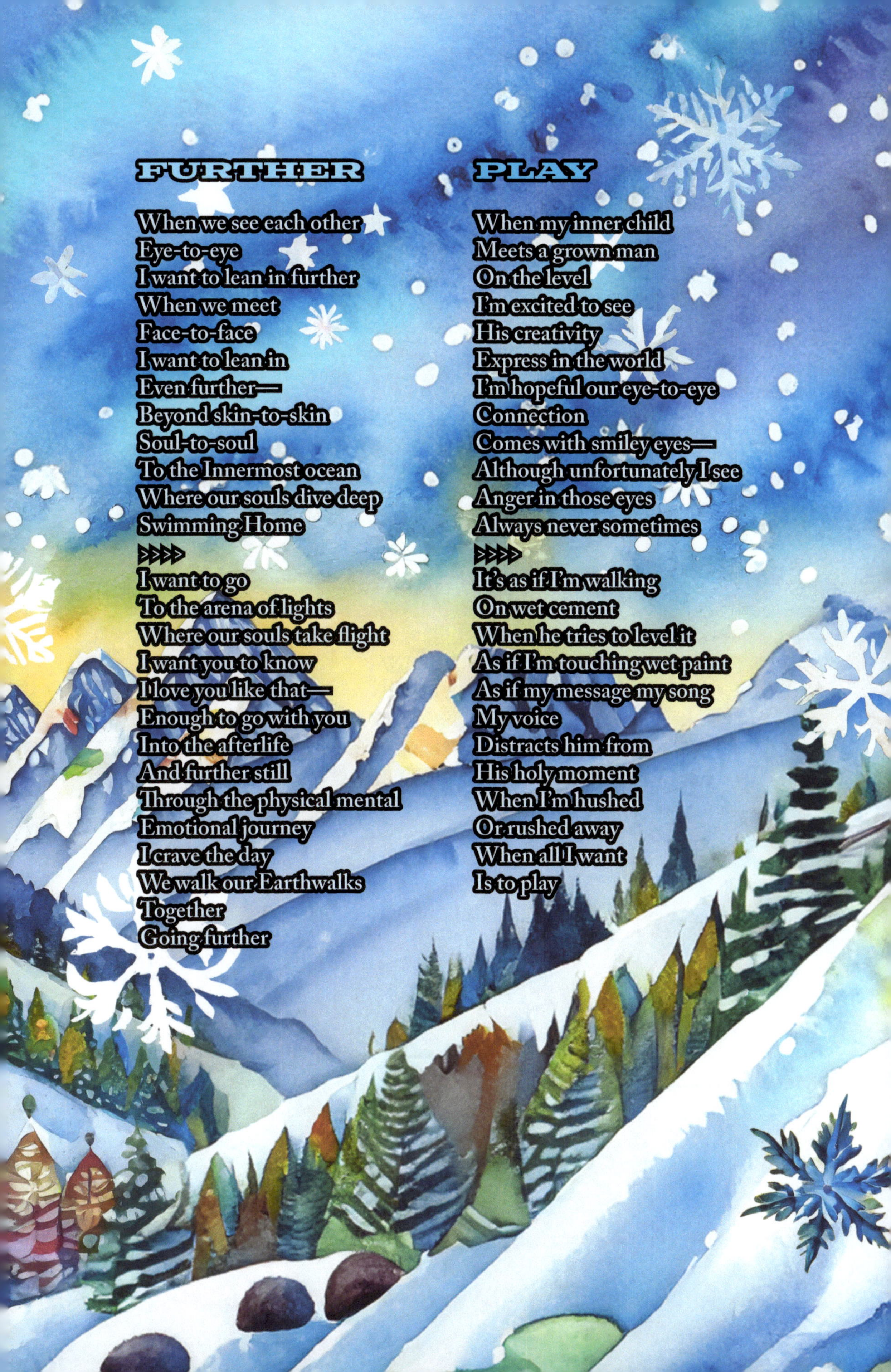

FURTHER

When we see each other
Eye-to-eye
I want to lean in further
When we meet
Face-to-face
I want to lean in
Even further—
Beyond skin-to-skin
Soul-to-soul
To the Innermost ocean
Where our souls dive deep
Swimming Home
▶▶▶▶
I want to go
To the arena of lights
Where our souls take flight
I want you to know
I love you like that—
Enough to go with you
Into the afterlife
And further still
Through the physical mental
Emotional journey
I crave the day
We walk our Earthwalks
Together
Going further

PLAY

When my inner child
Meets a grown man
On the level
I'm excited to see
His creativity
Express in the world
I'm hopeful our eye-to-eye
Connection
Comes with smiley eyes—
Although unfortunately I see
Anger in those eyes
Always never sometimes
▶▶▶▶
It's as if I'm walking
On wet cement
When he tries to level it
As if I'm touching wet paint
As if my message my song
My voice
Distracts him from
His holy moment
When I'm hushed
Or rushed away
When all I want
Is to play

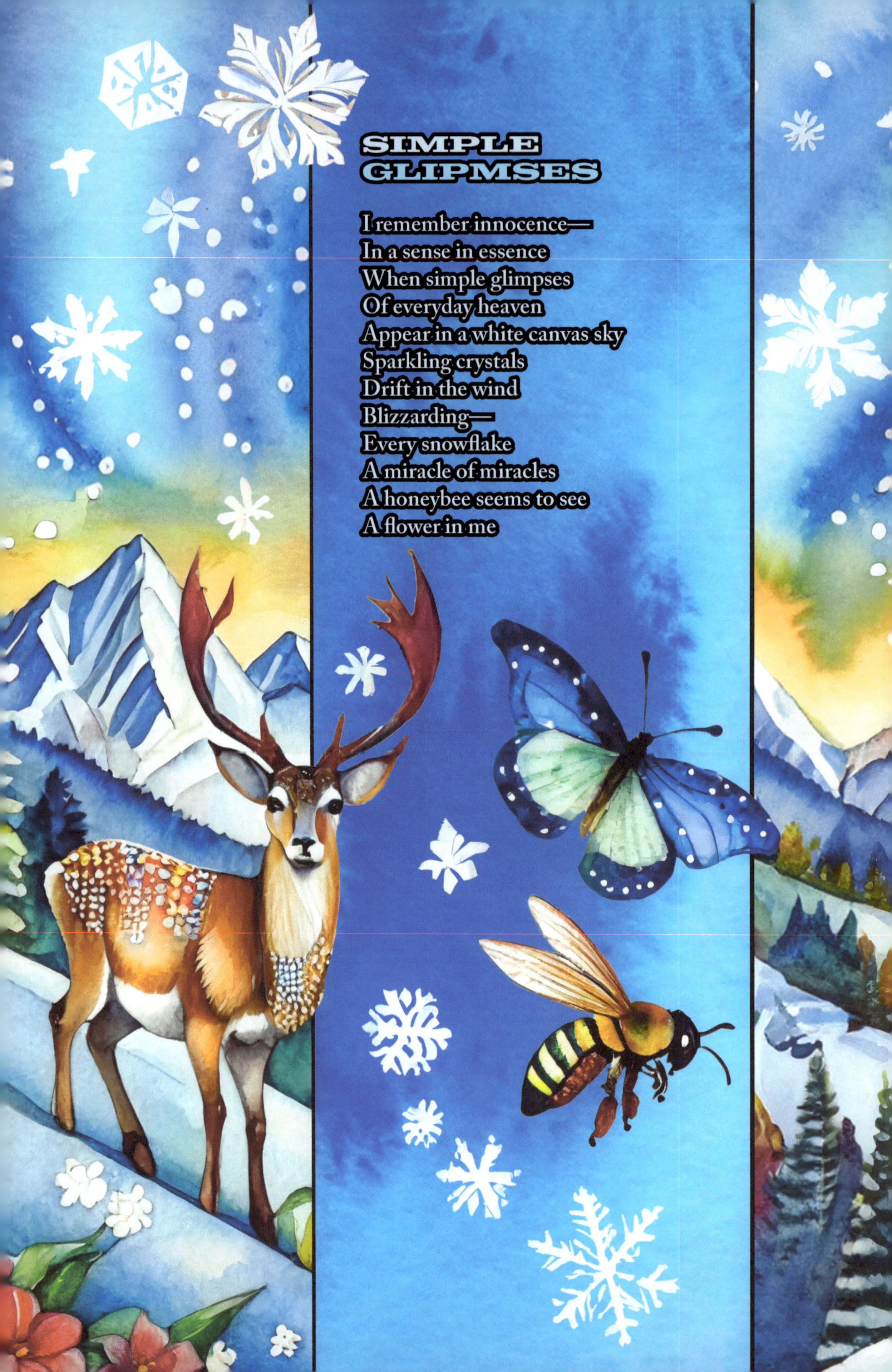

SIMPLE
GLIPMSES

I remember innocence—
In a sense in essence
When simple glimpses
Of everyday heaven
Appear in a white canvas sky
Sparkling crystals
Drift in the wind
Blizzarding—
Every snowflake
A miracle of miracles
A honeybee seems to see
A flower in me

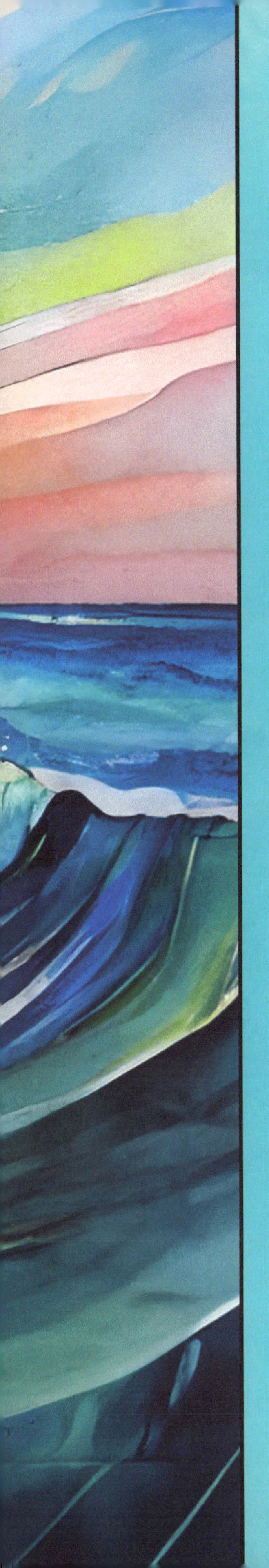
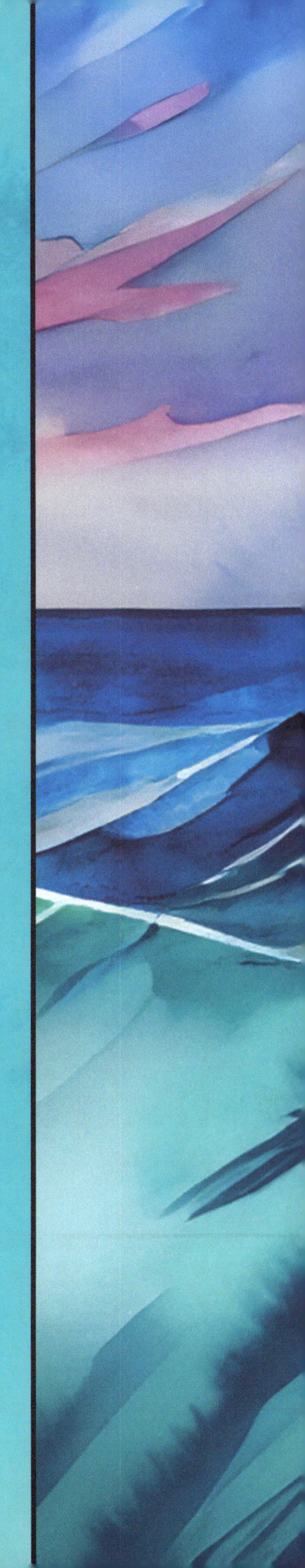

SHHH

In a sea of seas
Where seagulls chase the Sun
Over the horizon
I row my boat
On an open ocean
My heart remembers—
Love is a wave in motion
Wave after wave whispering
Shhhhhhh
Whales appear
Dolphins leap and dive
Seagulls by my side
All the while—
Shhh
My heart leaps
Remembering
Love makes me light
Shhhhhhhhhhhhhhhh
Hushing under us
Wavering wavering
Rippling rippling—
Shhhh
Rushing over us
Wavering wavering
Rippling rippling
Shhhhhh
Thundering over and under
Wavering wavering
Rippling rippling
Shhh
Touching all of us
Wavering wavering
Rippling rippling
Shhhhhhhhh

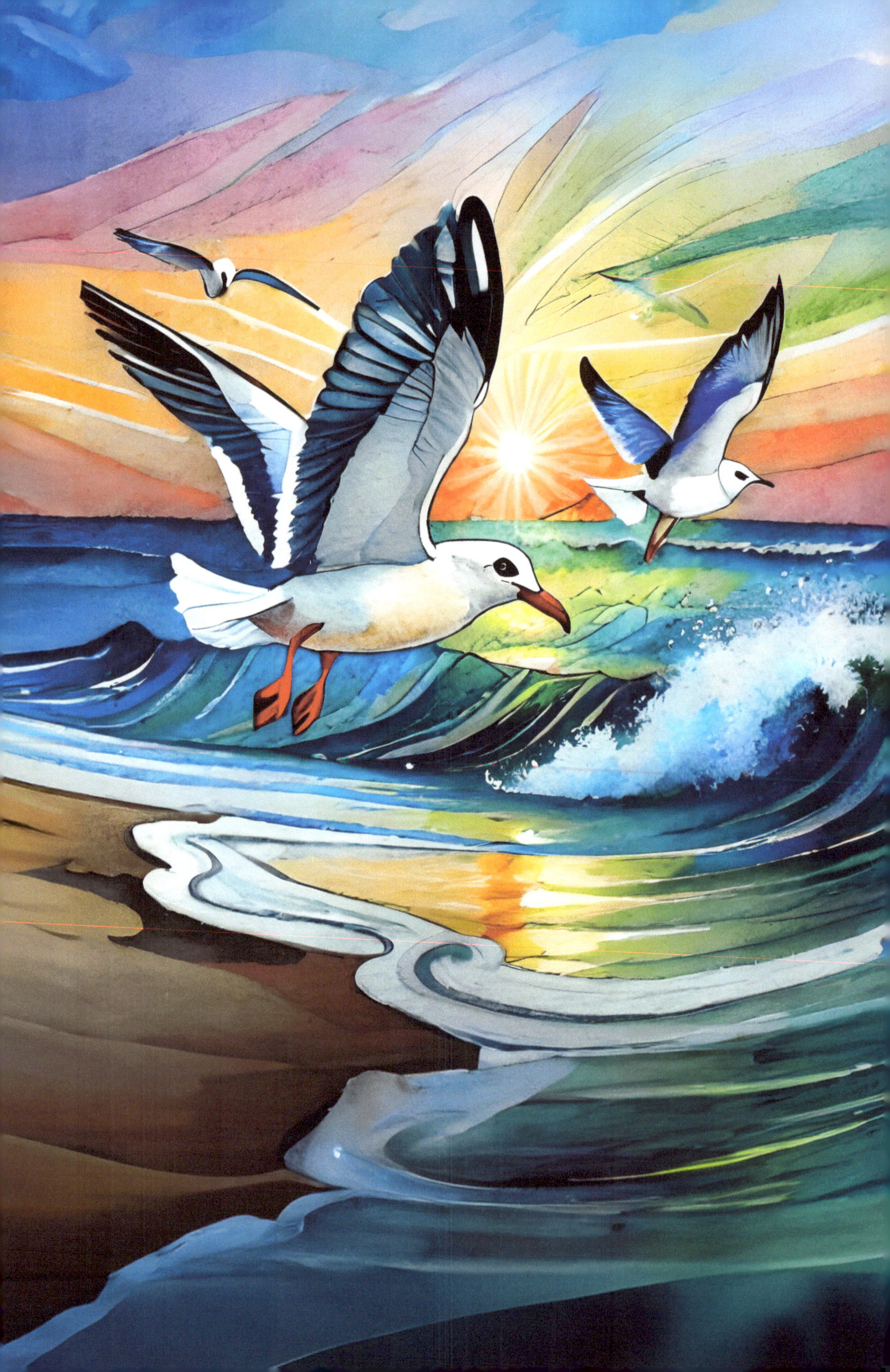

BRAVERY

Before I am a brother to all
I am a brother to one—
Wonderful brother
We try
To acclimate to worldly ways
Like other brothers
Following followers
Students of students
Imitators of imitators
Intimidated by differences
Irritated by disturbances
Afraid to fail—
Always never sometimes afraid
But we grow braver
Through each other's
Courage

SEA OF LOSS

At the risk of losing it all
We agree to win
In a sea of inevitable loss
Where tides rise water whirls
We lose ourselves
Our losses taking parts of our hearts
Far away
After too many tragedies
To hold a winning attitude
Too many truths to hold lies
We ask why—
Why are we here? Who are we now?
No one nowhere
Anyhow
We hold onto hope
To be Home

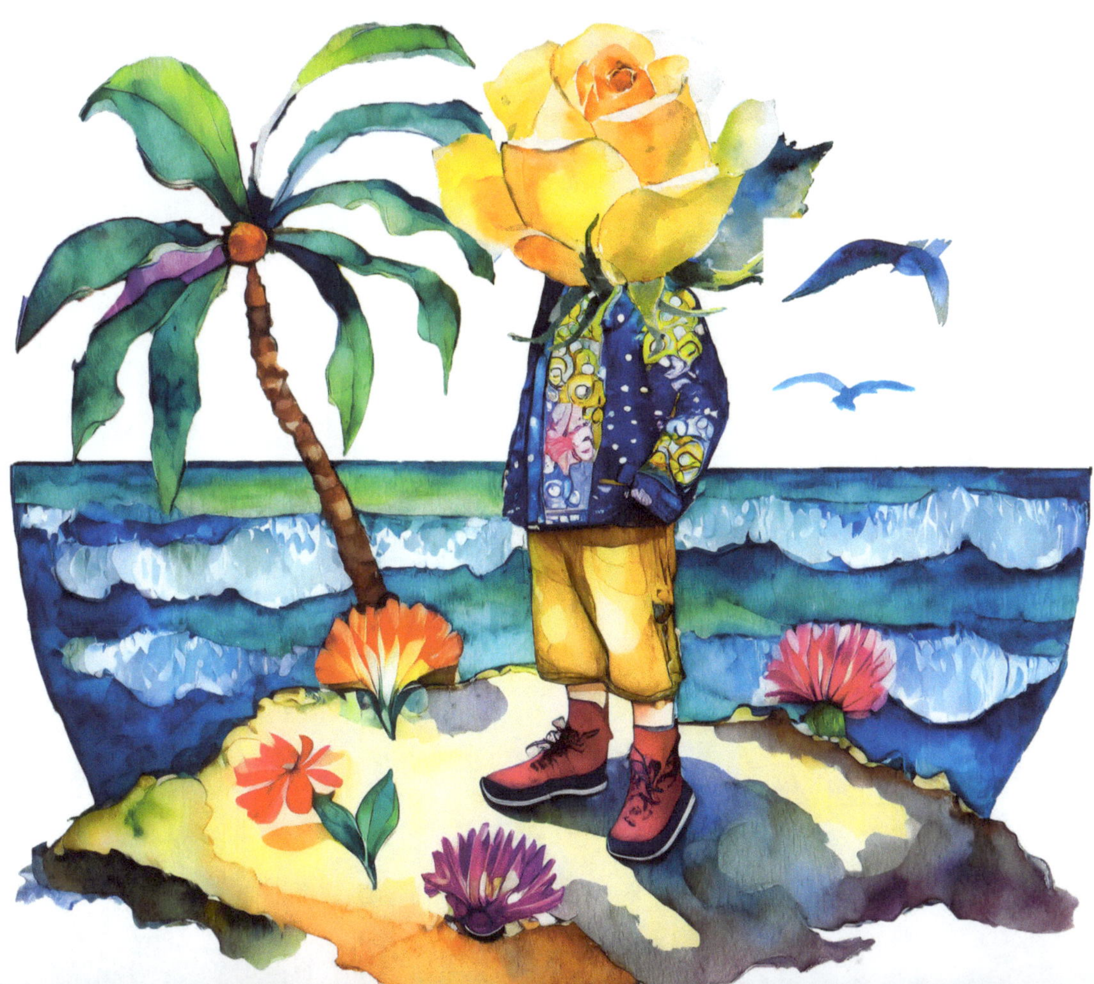

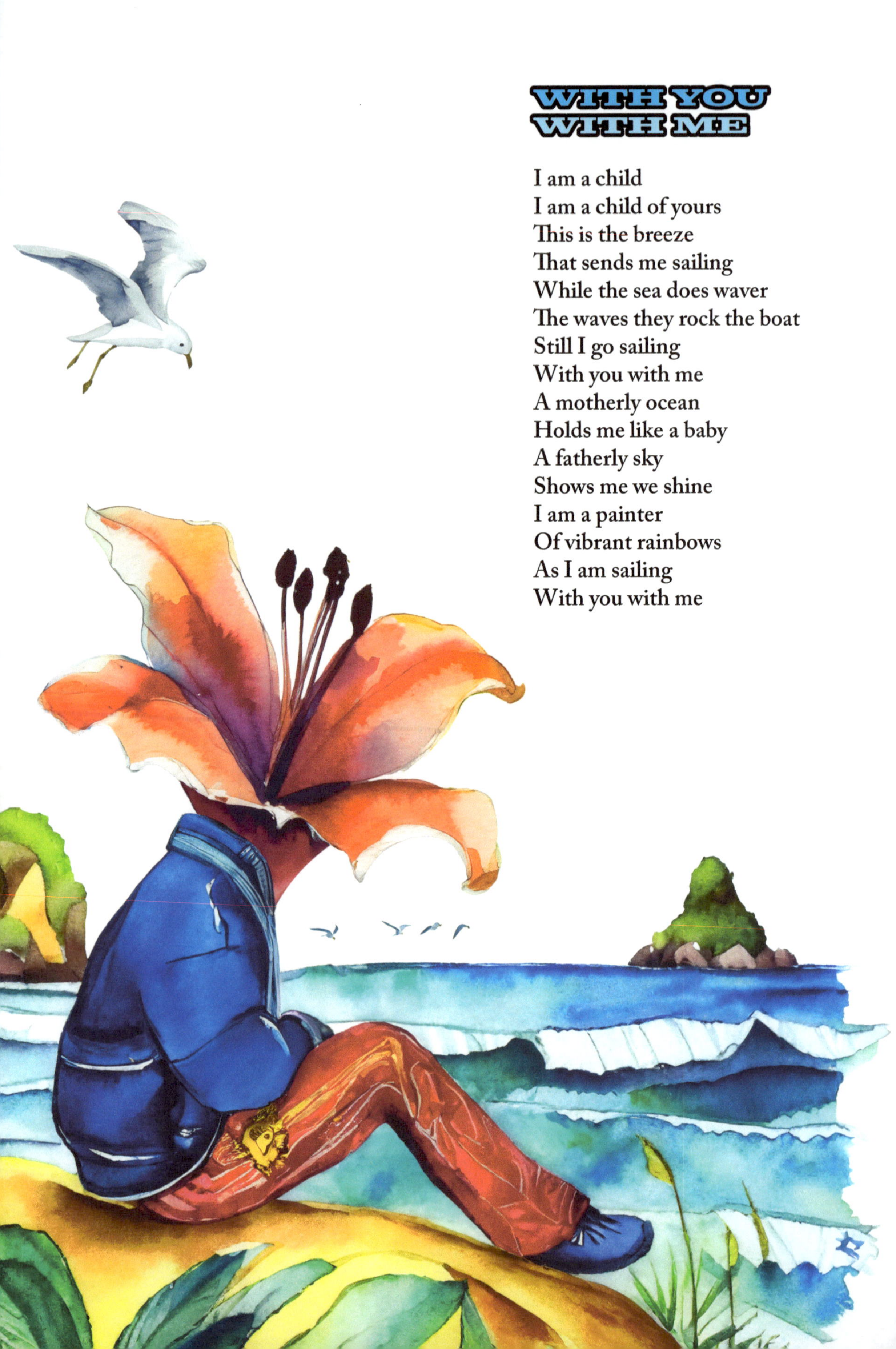

WITH YOU WITH ME

I am a child
I am a child of yours
This is the breeze
That sends me sailing
While the sea does waver
The waves they rock the boat
Still I go sailing
With you with me
A motherly ocean
Holds me like a baby
A fatherly sky
Shows me we shine
I am a painter
Of vibrant rainbows
As I am sailing
With you with me

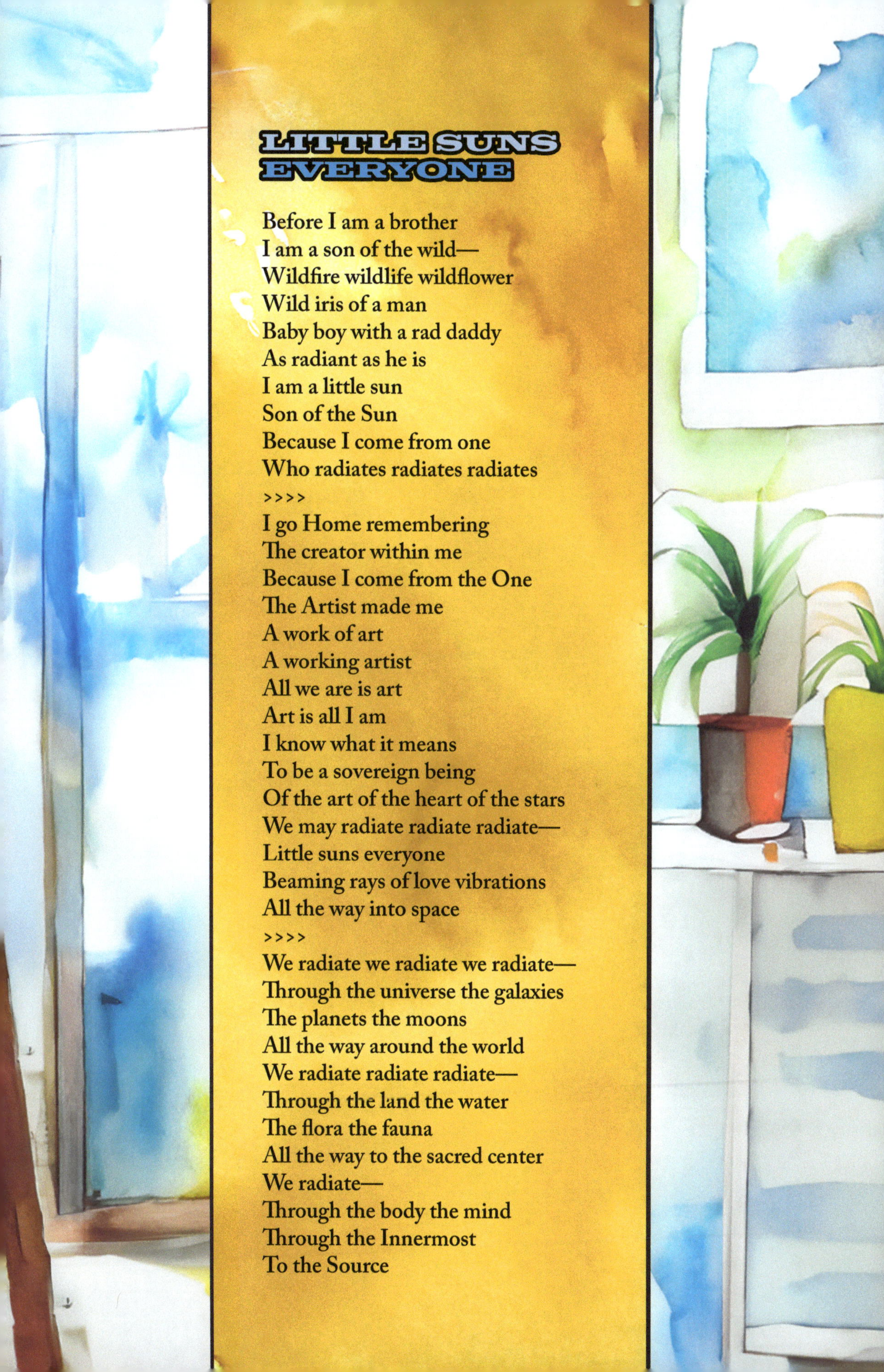

LITTLE SUNS
EVERYONE

Before I am a brother
I am a son of the wild—
Wildfire wildlife wildflower
Wild iris of a man
Baby boy with a rad daddy
As radiant as he is
I am a little sun
Son of the Sun
Because I come from one
Who radiates radiates radiates
>>>>
I go Home remembering
The creator within me
Because I come from the One
The Artist made me
A work of art
A working artist
All we are is art
Art is all I am
I know what it means
To be a sovereign being
Of the art of the heart of the stars
We may radiate radiate radiate—
Little suns everyone
Beaming rays of love vibrations
All the way into space
>>>>
We radiate we radiate we radiate—
Through the universe the galaxies
The planets the moons
All the way around the world
We radiate radiate radiate—
Through the land the water
The flora the fauna
All the way to the sacred center
We radiate—
Through the body the mind
Through the Innermost
To the Source

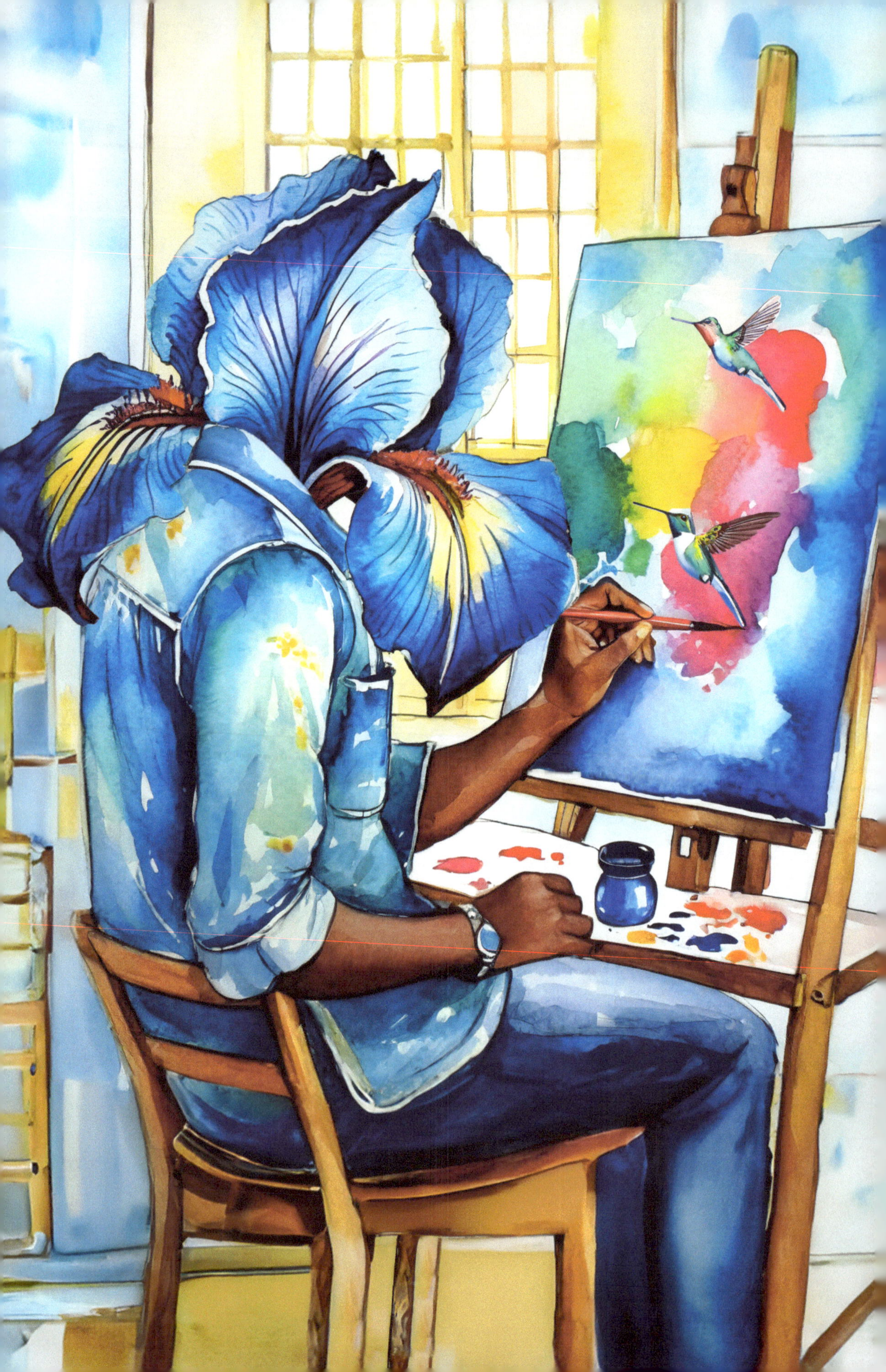

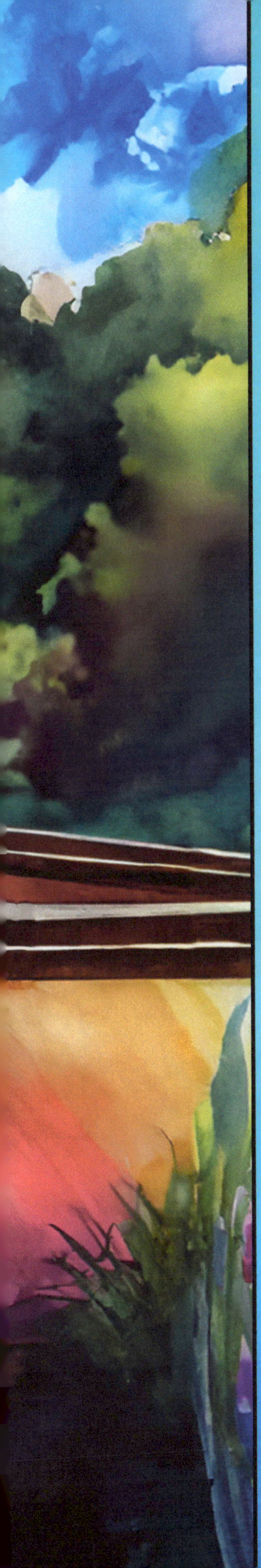

BEING A SON

In this instant
I expand my attention
To younger days
When I'm a little son
To a sunflower mother
Who plays Pachelbel
Ultra-slow
Inviting my attention in
When suddenly
The piano is a portal
To a Home beyond home—
A place that resonates
A space that radiates
> > > >
Like the Sun shines
The music radiates
Like the sunflower blooms
The music resonates
Like the Mom of all moms
My mom radiates radiates
She resonates resonates resonates
> > > >
I feel Home
As I listen now
Remembering those piano notes
Before I am a brother
I am a son
To a mother
Not only do I shine like one
I am—
A Sun
A son
Of a sunflower

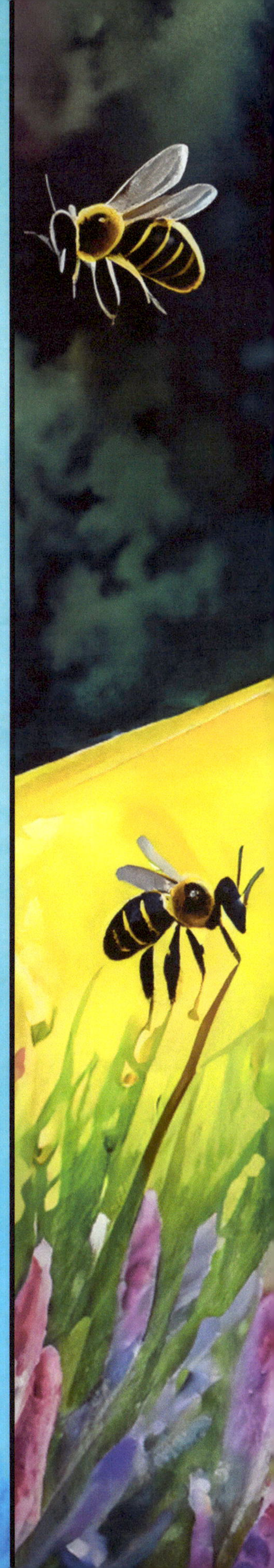

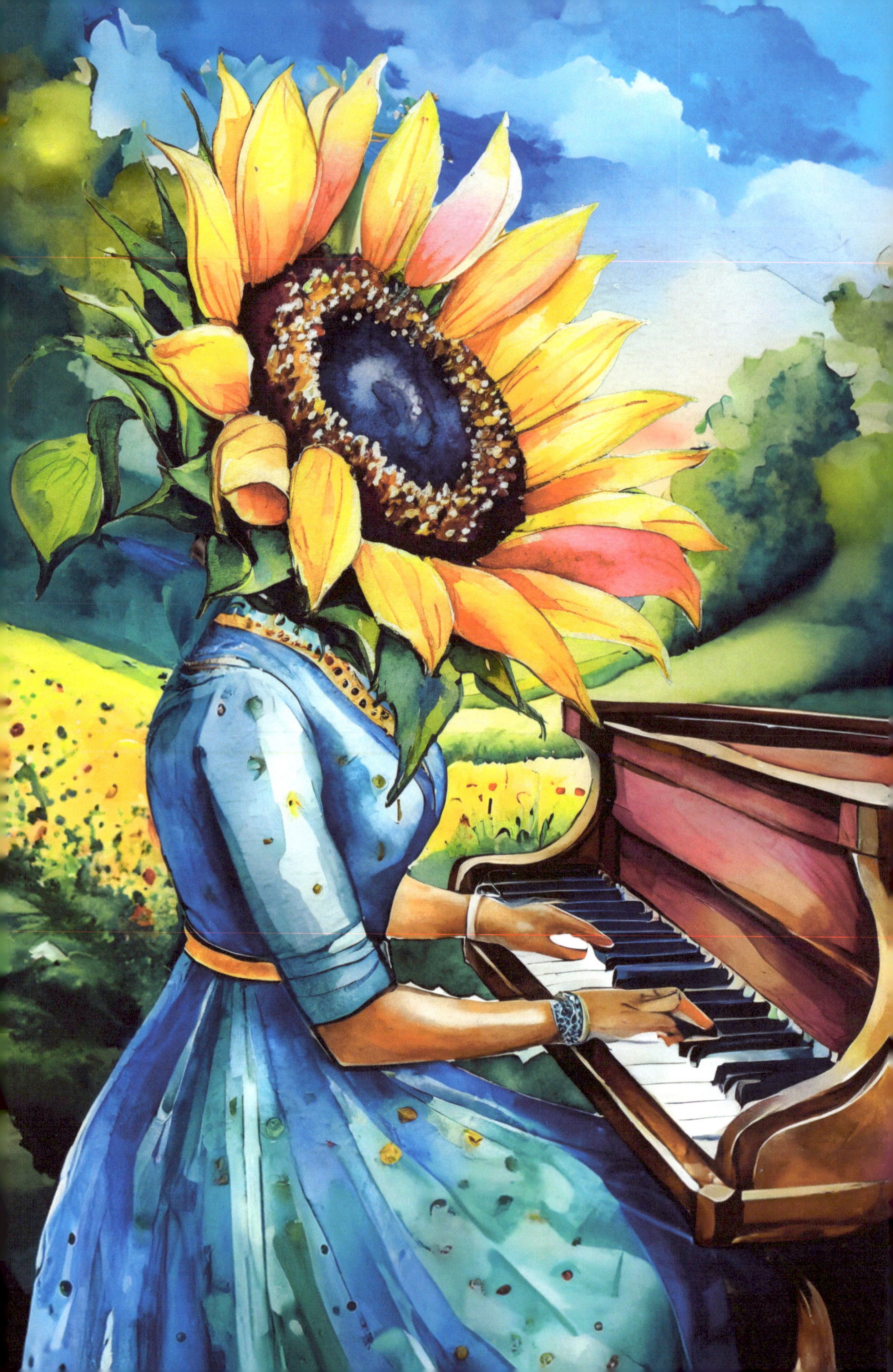

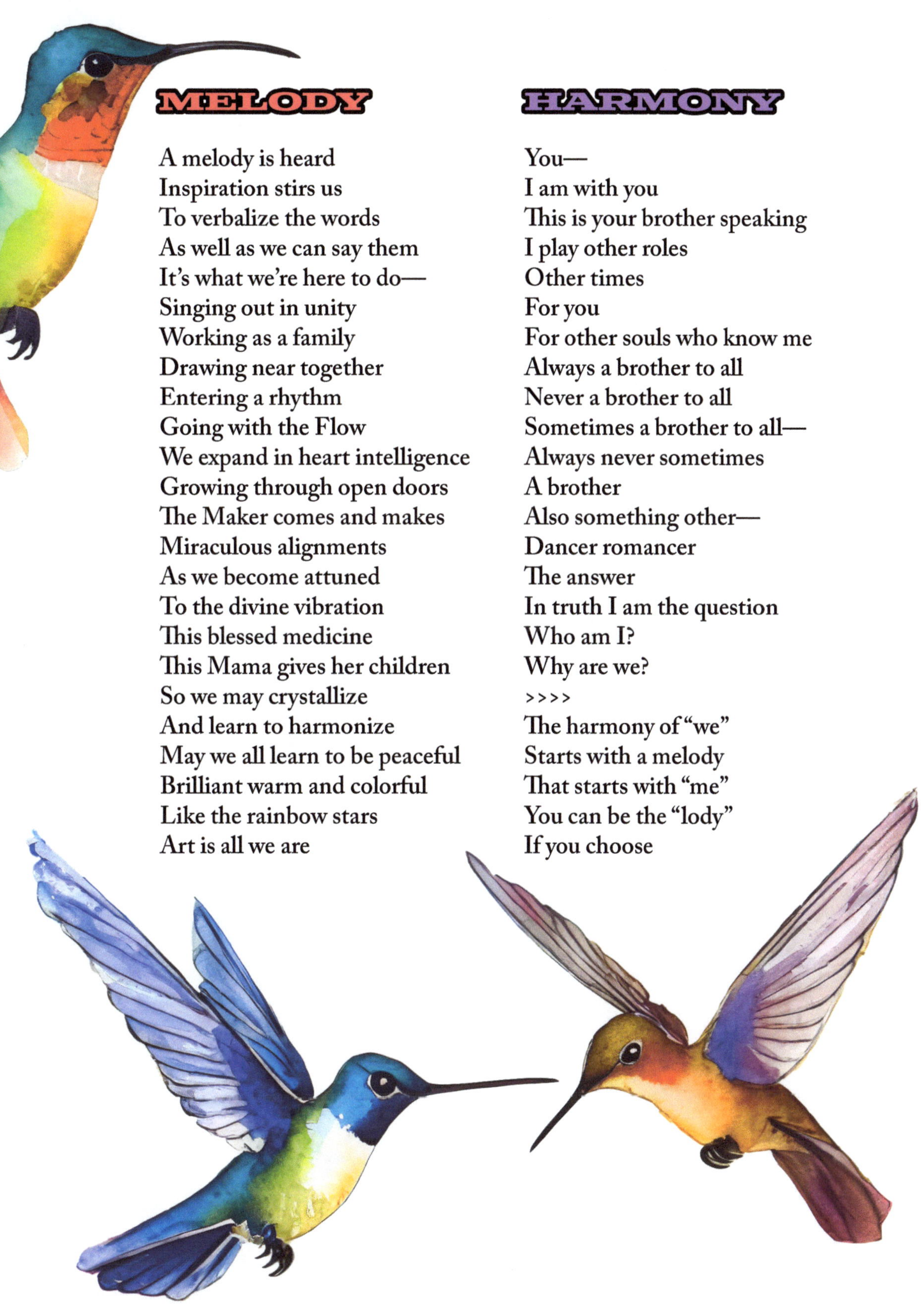

MELODY

A melody is heard
Inspiration stirs us
To verbalize the words
As well as we can say them
It's what we're here to do—
Singing out in unity
Working as a family
Drawing near together
Entering a rhythm
Going with the Flow
We expand in heart intelligence
Growing through open doors
The Maker comes and makes
Miraculous alignments
As we become attuned
To the divine vibration
This blessed medicine
This Mama gives her children
So we may crystallize
And learn to harmonize
May we all learn to be peaceful
Brilliant warm and colorful
Like the rainbow stars
Art is all we are

HARMONY

You—
I am with you
This is your brother speaking
I play other roles
Other times
For you
For other souls who know me
Always a brother to all
Never a brother to all
Sometimes a brother to all—
Always never sometimes
A brother
Also something other—
Dancer romancer
The answer
In truth I am the question
Who am I?
Why are we?
> > > >
The harmony of "we"
Starts with a melody
That starts with "me"
You can be the "lody"
If you choose

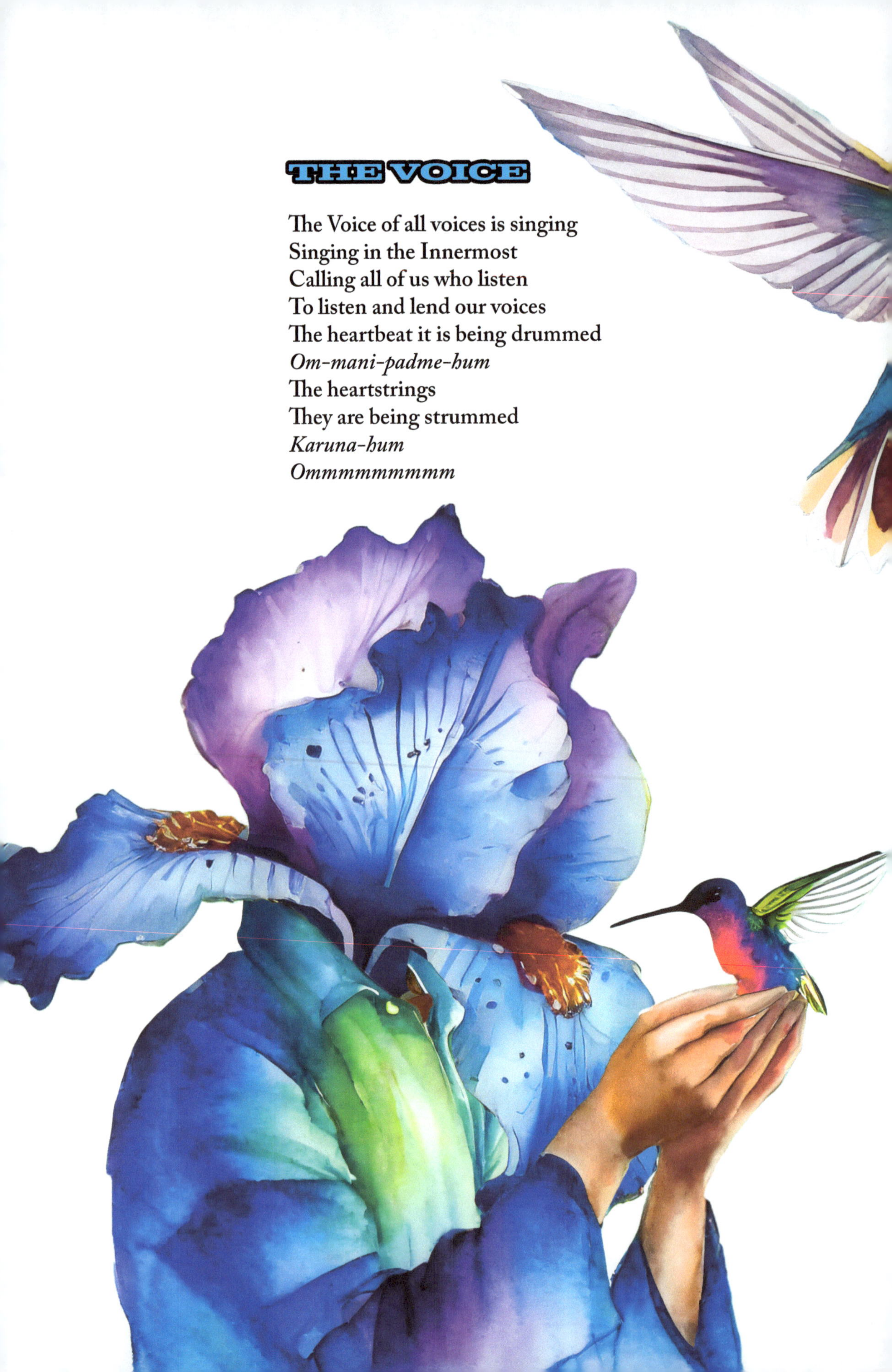

THE VOICE

The Voice of all voices is singing
Singing in the Innermost
Calling all of us who listen
To listen and lend our voices
The heartbeat it is being drummed
Om-mani-padme-hum
The heartstrings
They are being strummed
Karuna-hum
Ommmmmmmmm

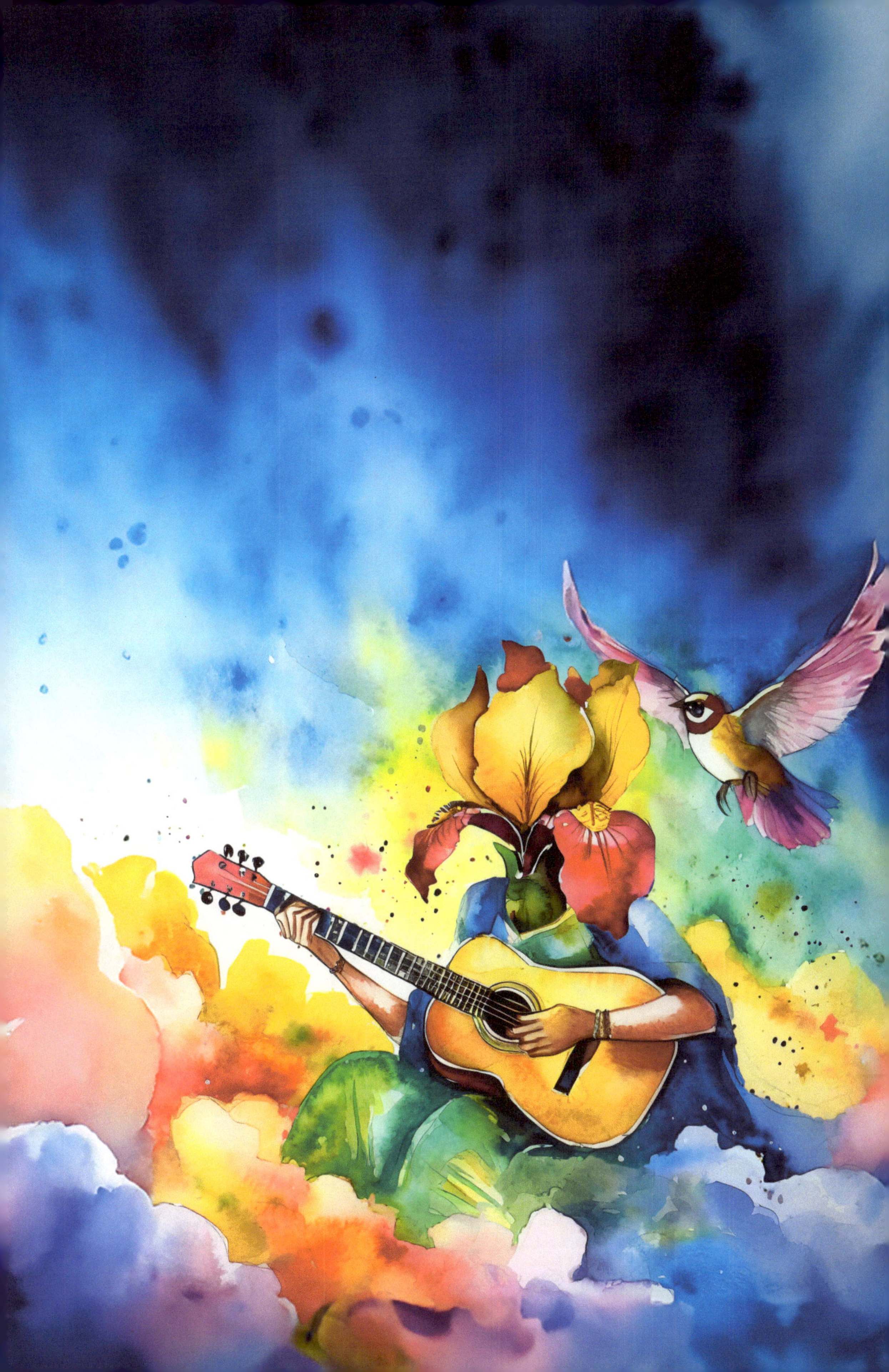

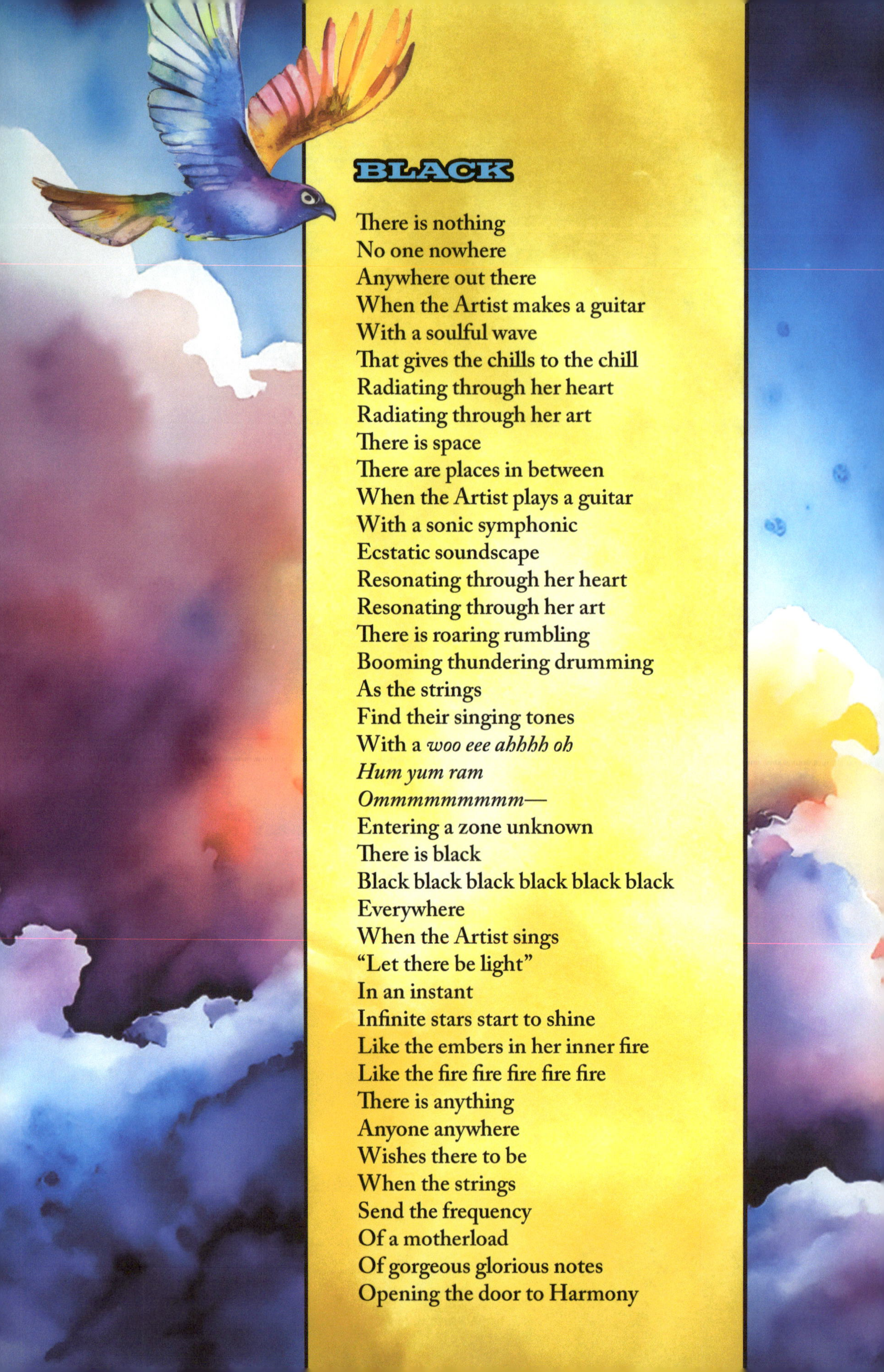
BLACK

There is nothing
No one nowhere
Anywhere out there
When the Artist makes a guitar
With a soulful wave
That gives the chills to the chill
Radiating through her heart
Radiating through her art
There is space
There are places in between
When the Artist plays a guitar
With a sonic symphonic
Ecstatic soundscape
Resonating through her heart
Resonating through her art
There is roaring rumbling
Booming thundering drumming
As the strings
Find their singing tones
With a woo eee ahhhh oh
Hum yum ram
Ommmmmmmmm—
Entering a zone unknown
There is black
Black black black black black black
Everywhere
When the Artist sings
"Let there be light"
In an instant
Infinite stars start to shine
Like the embers in her inner fire
Like the fire fire fire fire fire
There is anything
Anyone anywhere
Wishes there to be
When the strings
Send the frequency
Of a motherload
Of gorgeous glorious notes
Opening the door to Harmony

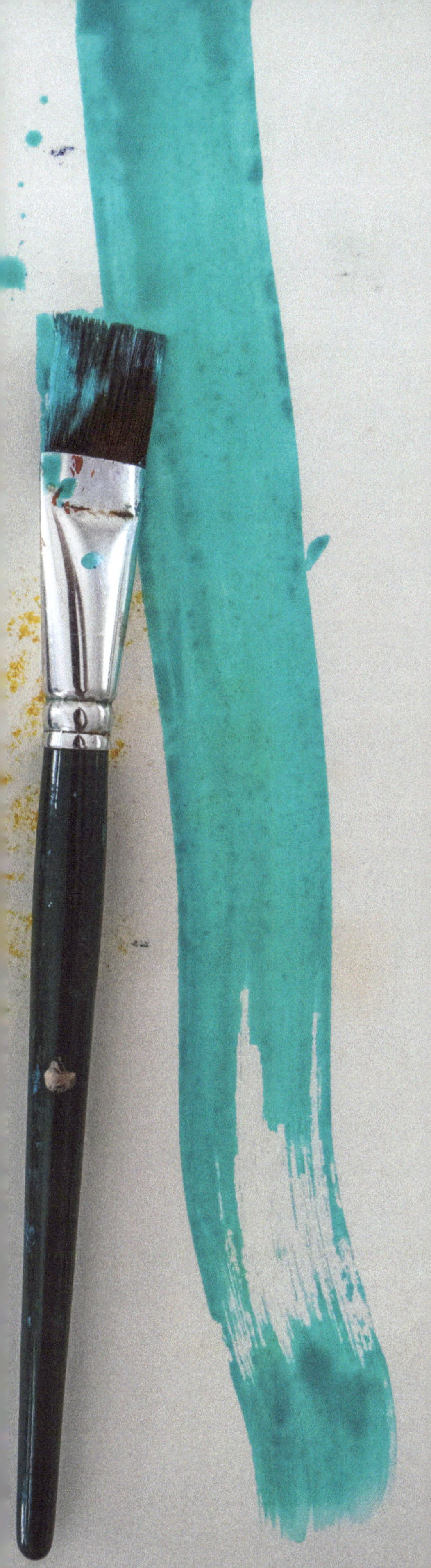

FLOWER PEOPLE

Always never sometimes
I wonder—
Am I becoming a plant?
When I lay down roots
When I bloom
Will I produce the fruits
To draw the bees
To spread the seeds
To flourish forever?
In open fields
Where aspens and mycelium
Interconnect
One living organism
Growing together—
Where do I grow from there?
Where do I become we?
Meanwhile
The raindrop that is me
Blends into the sea
Becoming one
Meanwhile
The ember I am
Blazes in a bonfire
Meanwhile
The rosebud I am
Grows on a rosebush
Part of a greater whole
Connected to the dirt
Sharing common ground
With all life
I am you are
Weeeeee
Swaying as grass blades
In a field of feelings
We feel the petals
The thorns of life
Flower people
Blooming where we are planted

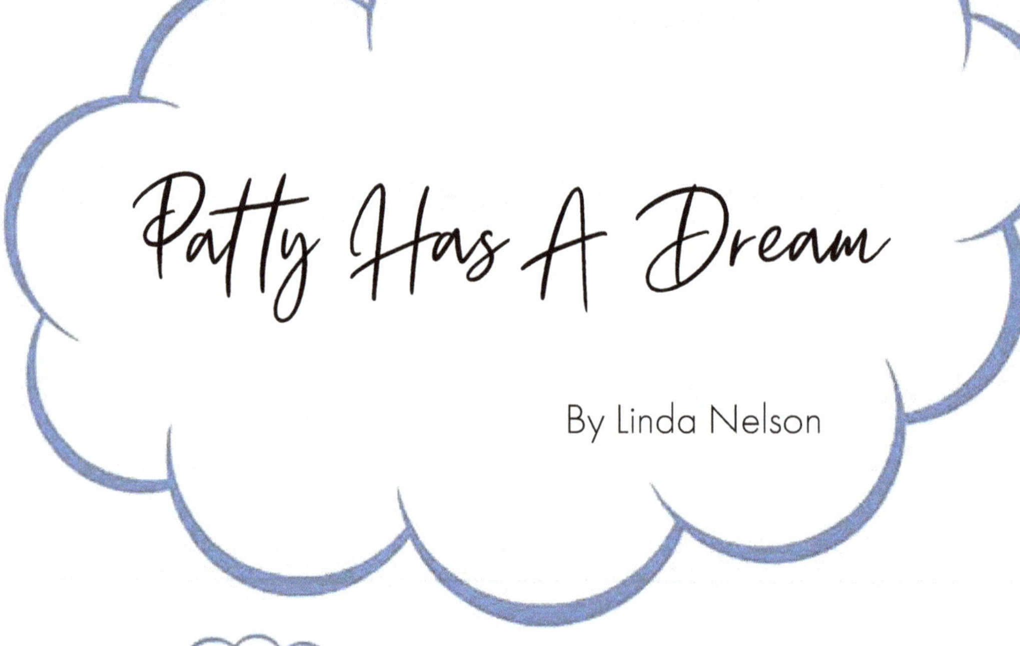

Patty Has A Dream
By Linda Nelson

This book is dedicated to my grandchildren:

Taylor, Joseph, Holden, Ava, and Austin whom I love very much

One day Patty and Gus were taking their morning walk. Patty told Gus she had a most unusual dream. Gus asked her what was it about. She told him that they had left the campus and decided to travel around the world.

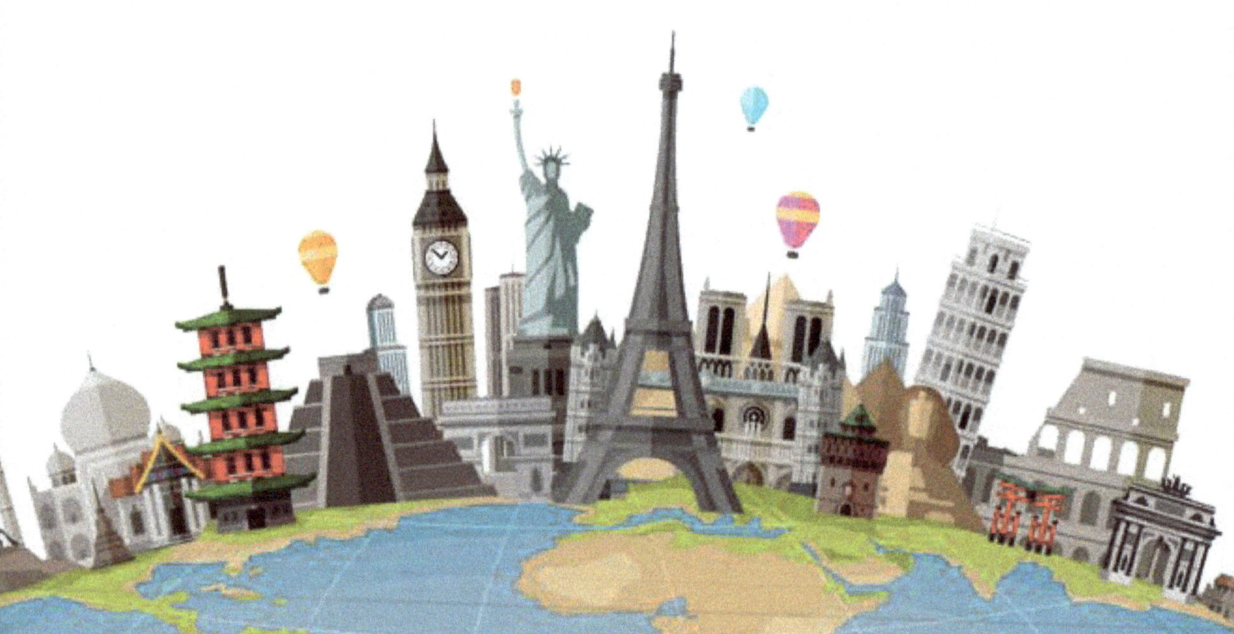

Gus was very interested. He had always thought about leaving but knew how he loved his friends and most of all Patty.

He asked her about her dream in more detail. She said they left the campus at night so as not to let the insert Patty and Gus leaving others know of their plan. The squirrels would wonder what happened to them but they would be back before they were missed that much.

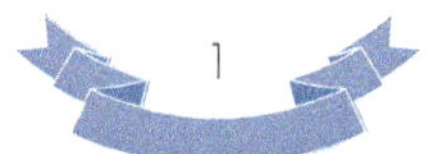

Patty and Gus got to the train station and took a train South.

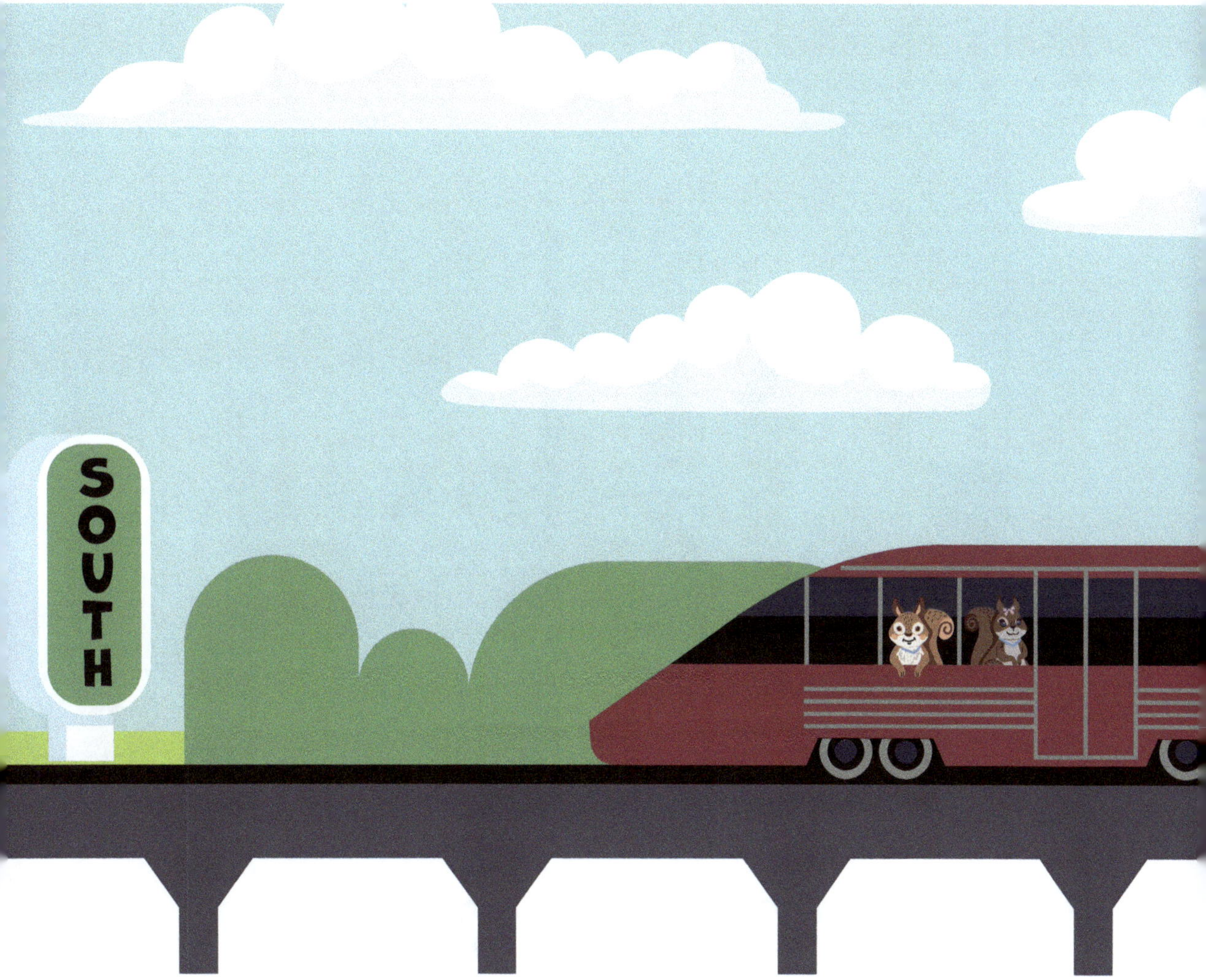

They traveled through the southern states, South Carolina, Georgia, Florida, Louisiana,

Alabama, Mississippi and Arkansas.

The weather was warm and pleasant, they loved it.

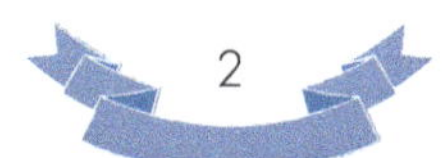

Patty said every state was so beautiful that she wanted to stay longer in each place. In her dream they came across so many wonderful people who stopped and fed them and played with them. It was a happy time, mostly because they were together. However, all the people wondered about their **BLUE RIBBONS** and tried to untie them and they would have to run away. This made them feel bad, even though they knew no one wanted to hurt them.

As they traveled back North, the weather became much colder something they were not used to seeing. They traveled to Pennsylvania, New Jersey, New York, Connecticut, Massachusetts, Rhode Island, Vermont, New Hampshire and Maine.

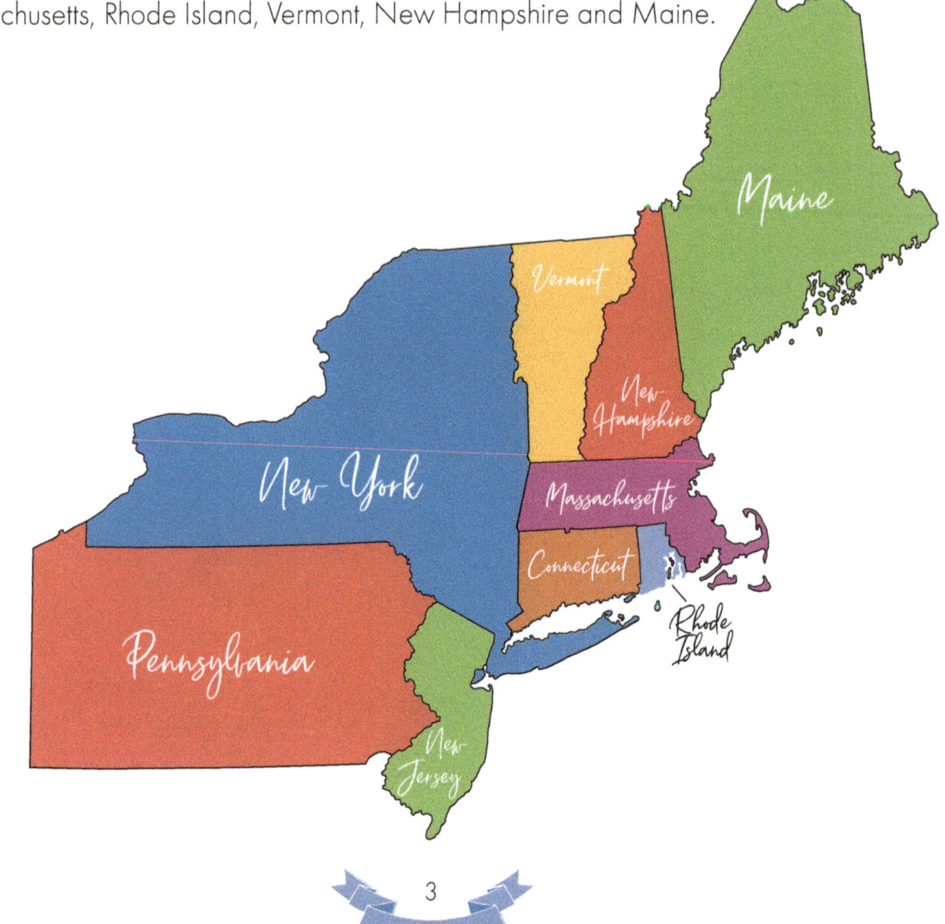

They saw this white rain coming down from the sky but did not know what it was. It covered all the streets and houses. Patty had read about this white rain and said they call it snow.

They saw children making all kinds of things out of the snow. The children laid in the snow and put their arms out and moved their legs back and forth they looked very funny. Gus and Patty did the same and had such a fun time with this new game.

When the children noticed them, they started playing with them and rolling snowballs at them to play. Gus and Patty joined them and everyone was having such a good time they forgot how cold it was.

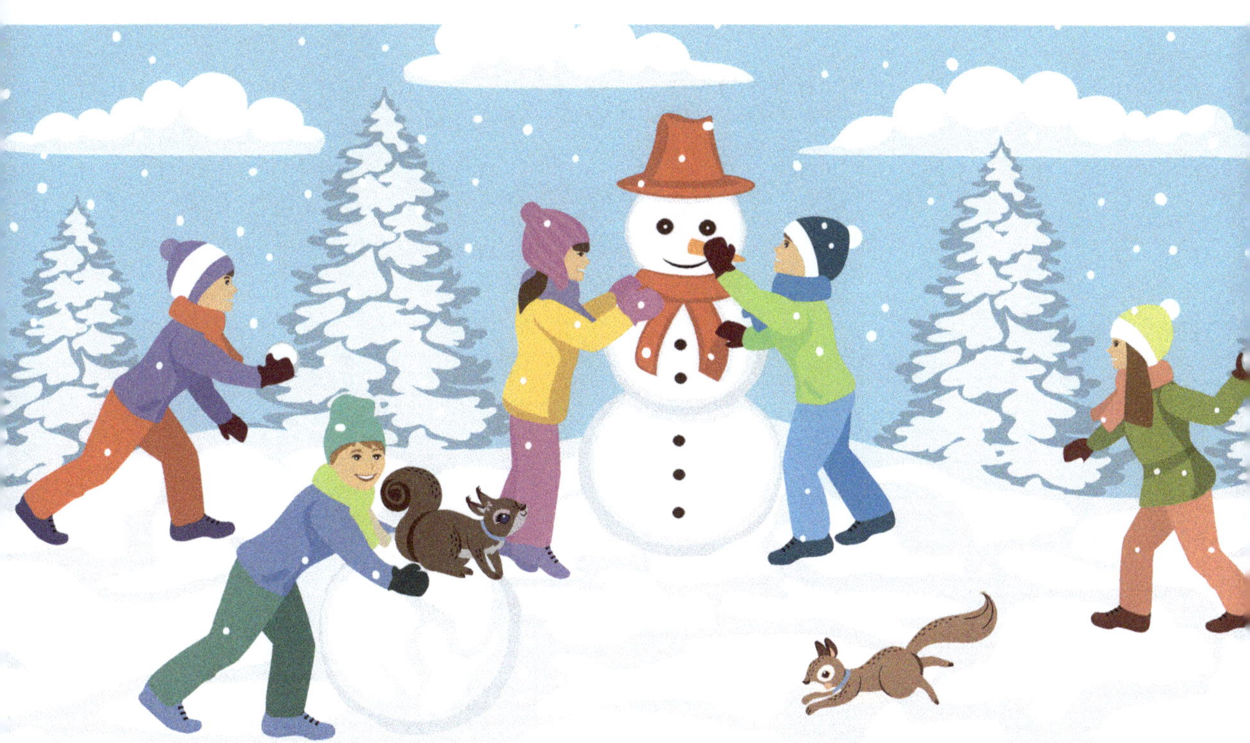

They made friends with the children and remembered how much they missed Joy and

Hero. Everyone they met seemed to love them and they were so happy to be with them.

It only made it harder to move on.

They started traveling again. This time to the West where the weather was a bit better.

They traveled West to Montana, Idaho, Colorado, Wyoming, Nebraska, North Dako-

ta, South Dakota, Arizona and New Mexico. Everywhere was so beautiful with its trees

and green grass and beautiful houses. Anyone who lives here should love all its beauty.

They stayed here for a while since there were so many trees where no one would bother

them. Also, there were plenty of nuts to store if they decided to stay longer than they had

planned.

After a few weeks of enjoying this change they decided to move once again. This time

to the Pacific States. Washington, Oregon and California. What would they find there?

Each state was more beautiful than the one before and they just loved being together to

be able to share this wonderful memory. There were many horses and the most beautiful

water they had ever seen. People kept asking about their **BLUE RIBBONS** but by now

they were used to this. They were just so proud to have them because it meant that they

had a home.

They had heard about a place called Alaska where it was so cold that people lived in something called an Igloo. What was that like?

Patty was always reading about travel and told Gus it was a house made out of ice. She also told him that people would ice fish from inside them sometime. Gus was so interested in what Patty had to say. She was so smart. He loved that about her. They decided to go to Alaska. It would be a very long way but they had seen so much and why stop now.

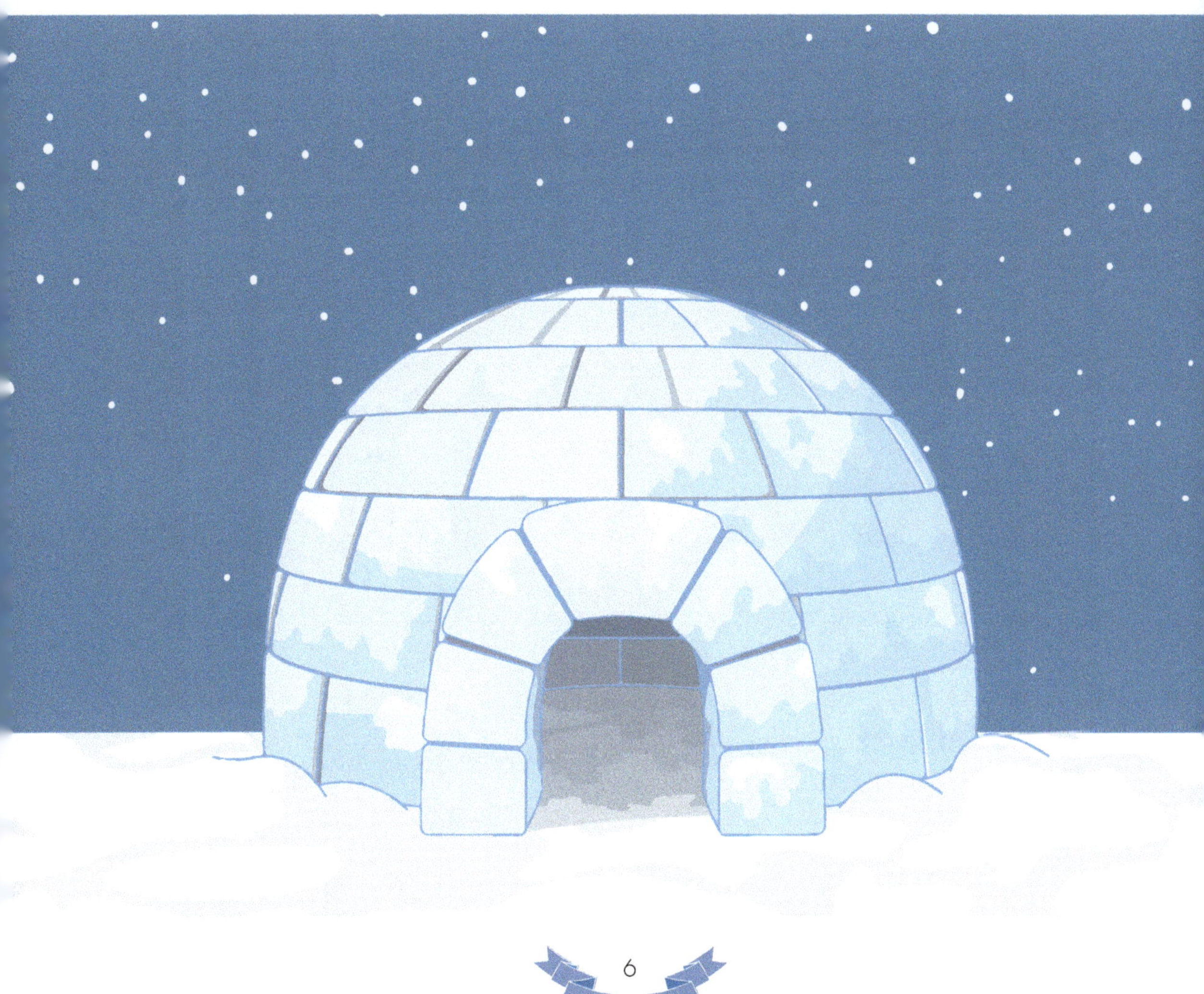

When they arrived in Alaska, they noticed some very strange buildings just as Patty had

said.

They decided to go over and touch one, it was all made of ice just as Patty had read.

They had never seen anything like it. Then a man came out of one of them dressed in winter

clothes to keep warm. It was very cold. Patty snuggled very close to Gus and suddenly

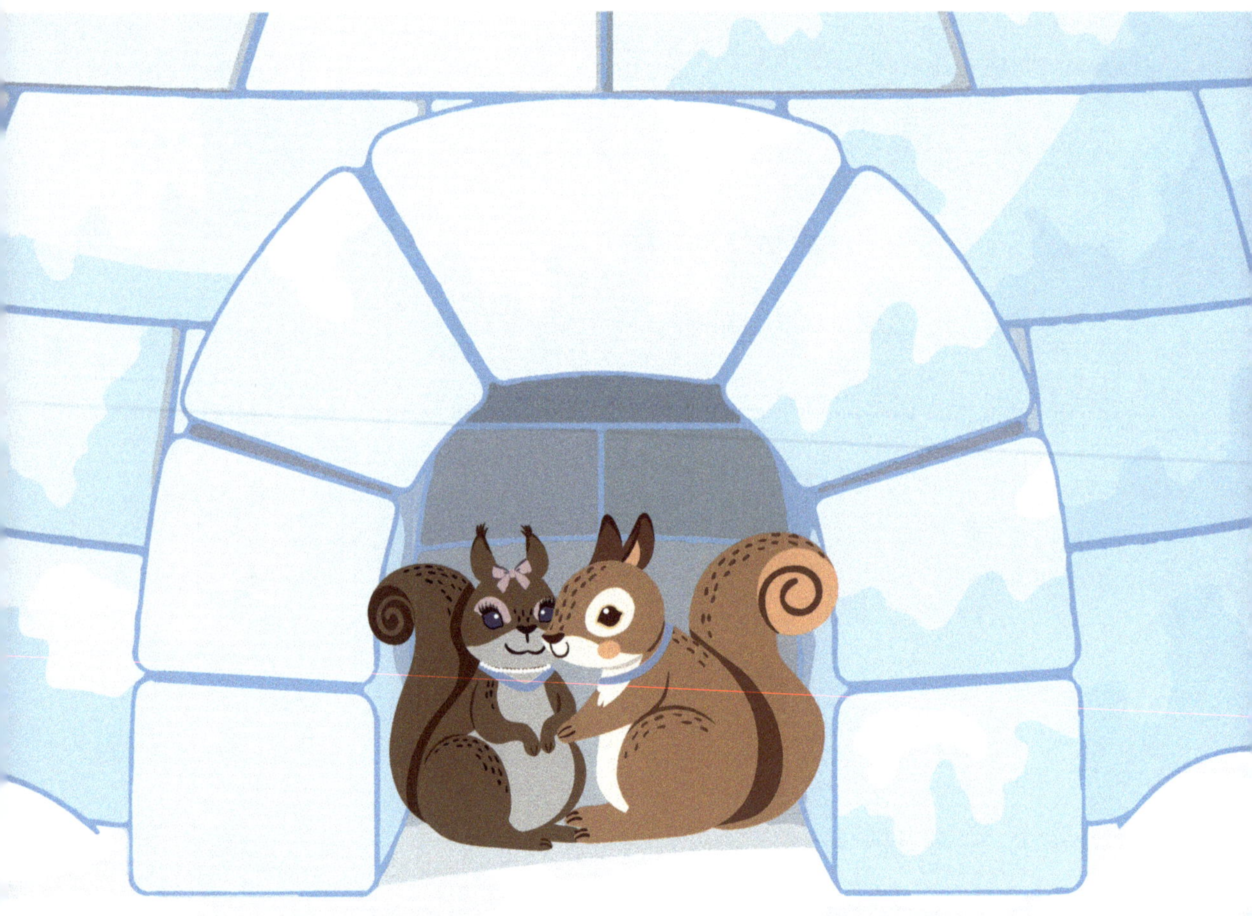

the man from the hut was snuggling with another person to keep warm. Gus and Patty both

knew this was the right way to keep warm in Alaska.

They were having a lot of fun but it was time to leave and so very cold. They still had

one last place to visit. It took longer than anywhere else but the beauty of Hawaii was

the best of all. When they arrived, the weather was sunny and clear, you could see the

bottom of the ocean and the water was blue like the sky. Patty said how could anyone

every want to leave this place? Gus agreed. The people were all wearing flowers

around their necks, Patty asked Gus to find out why. They found a group of people

sitting and eating and laughing.

This would be a great place to find some food. Everyone was laughing and dancing

so Patty and Gus decided to do the same. Suddenly, they were noticed and people tried

to pick them up. Patty and Gus were so scared. The people were so gentle and gave them

food to eat and started playing with them. They kept touching their **BLUE RIBBONS**

and gave them one made of flowers.

Then other squirrels came to join them. These squirrels looked a little like them but had

a different color. They were grey. Patty and Gus were brown. The squirrels were friendly.

Told Patty and Gus that squirrels from different parts of the WORLD are different colors to

protect them from the sun and enemies that might want to hurt them. Gus and Patty knew about that but were not at all worried. They were safe at home and always would be.

Gus and Patty were having such a good time with their new friends that they did not realize they had been gone for three months. Patty told Gus that everyone they knew back home was probably worried about them and trying to find them. Gus asked if there was a way to get a letter to Joy or one of the other students on campus. Joy was there only hope. How were they going to find someone to get a letter to Joy? This was the biggest problem facing Gus and Patty.

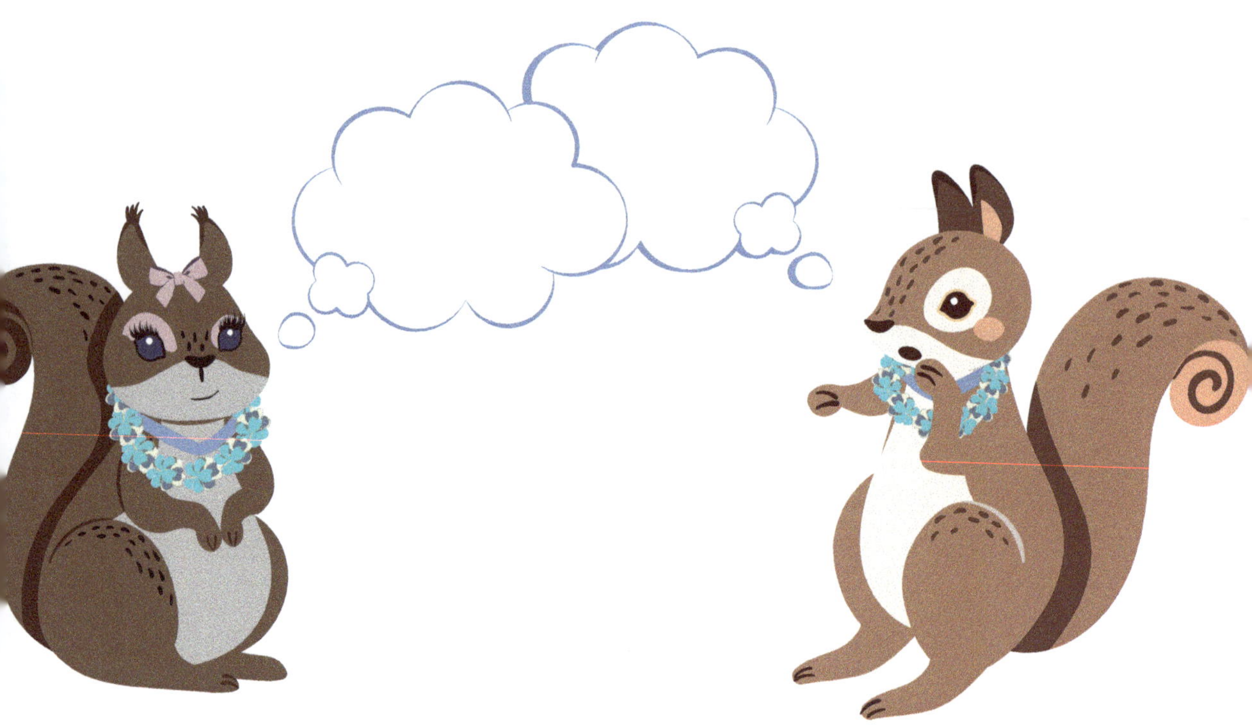

After many days they had no luck getting the attention of adults. Patty told Gus they would just have to make the trip back to the home they loved so much. Gus was not happy about the long travel back. They were so lucky to have made this trip around the world and learned and seen so much. Now going back would be difficult.

They hoped the flowers that were given to them by the people of Hawaii would be a good luck piece hoping to bring them home safely. They started to look for a train the way but there were none available. Most people in Hawaii travel by boat. Since Squirrels do not like water this was something, they had to think about.

Patty started to cry and said this was a terrible idea we should never have left our home and our friends. Gus held Patty and told her not to cry they would make it back safe. They just had to come up with a plan.

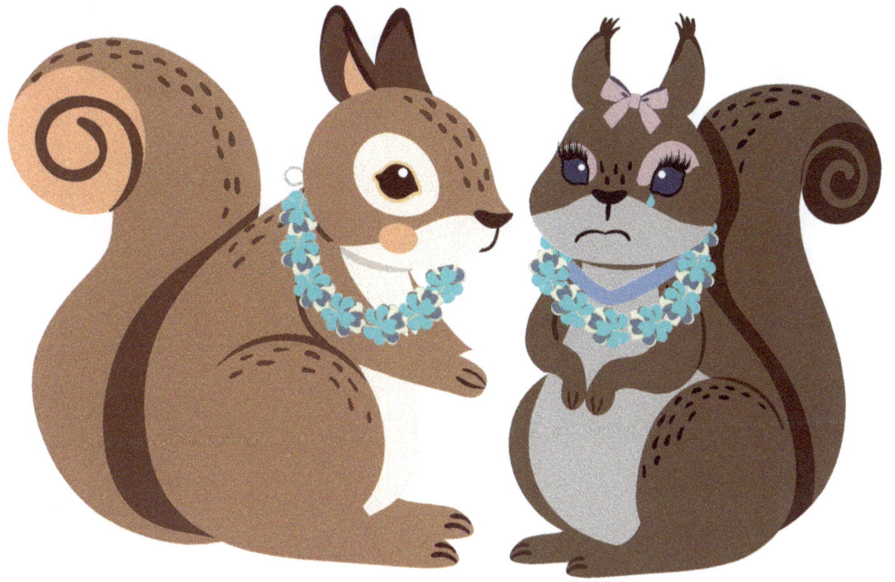

After a few days Gus came up with a plan. They would go down by the water and see

if they could get onto a boat and just hope it takes them to land where they could find

a train. Patty said, "This was a lot to hope for". Gus told her they had their flowers

necklace and their **BLUE RIBBON** to keep them safe.

Finally, after many days they were able to get on a boat. Patty was so scared that she

almost fell overboard when she ran to get on. They sat together for what seemed to be

days but was actually ours. Suddenly the boat stopped and they ran off. They were in the

busiest area they had ever seen, even on the first day of school it was never as busy as this.

People everywhere. They had to run as fast as they could not get stepped on.

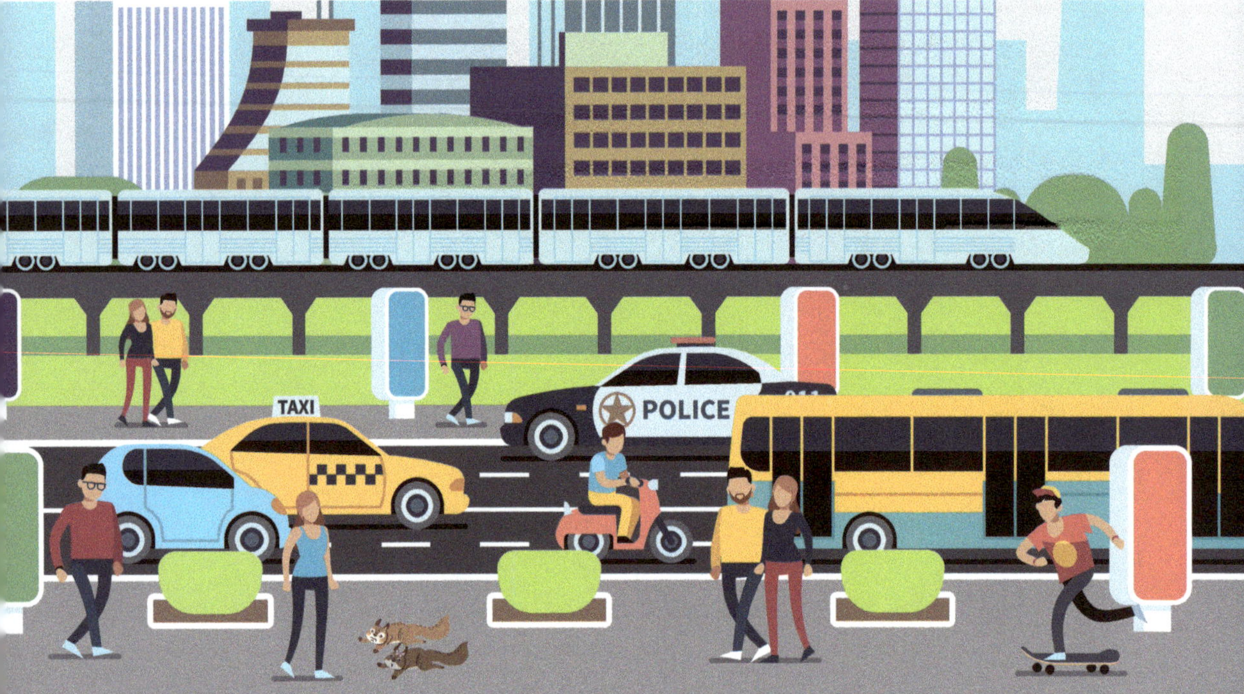

They kept running and running until they could not run any more. Just when they

were about to stop, they saw a train coming. They could not believe their eyes.

Quickly they jumped on the train and for now they were safe.

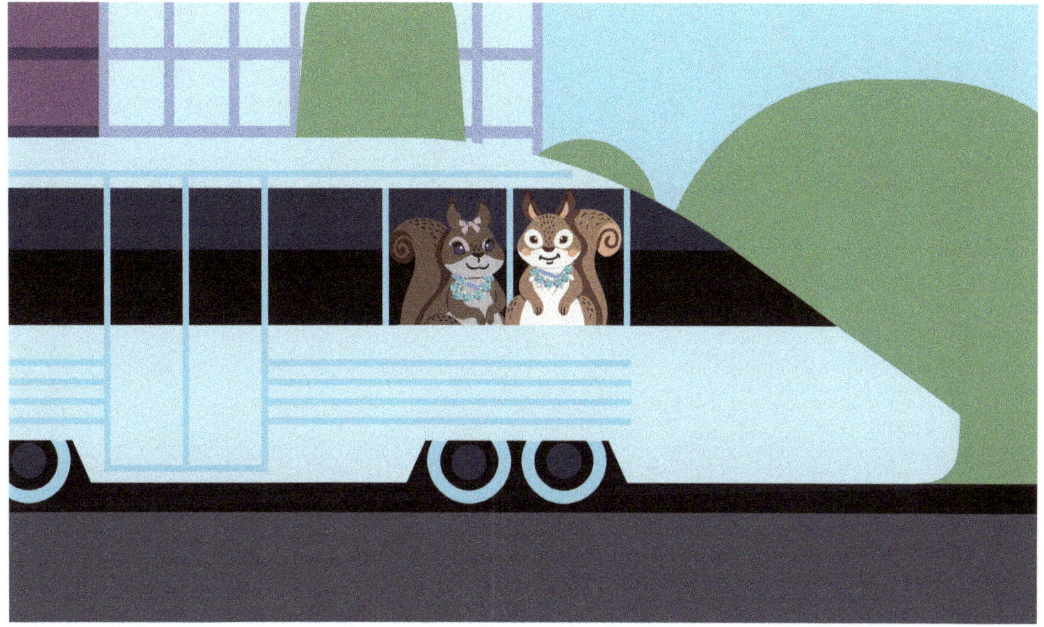

Patty asked Gus where is the train going, I'm so scared. Gus told her not to worry he

would try and find out and that she should try and get some rest. Gus decided to get some

much-needed rest as well. After a very long time, it was actually days the train stopped.

Patty and Gus woke up and were so very hungry. They realized they had slept for days.

They could not believe it. They went into the dining car of the train where Gus hoped to

find food. He was right, there was. He and Patty were able to fill their stomachs and felt

so much better.

In fact, they felt just great. Gus saw the train had stopped near a beautiful area with large oak tree. His tree was an oak tree so he knew the smell. He wanted to tell Patty but she had found her favorite food a chocolate chip cookie so he decided to see where they were by himself. How far could they have come when they lost track of time? Gus decided to take a better look, so he peeked out the window and saw something so familiar that he could not believe his eyes. It was the light on the campus entrance. He started jumping up and down and running around with joy that for the moment he forgot Patty. He was just about to jump off the train when he realized. As quickly as he could he ran to get her just as the train was about to pull away. Gus saw Patty just in time to say JUMP.

She had a mouth full of cookie crumbs but did just that. When the train pulled away and they were standing by the campus entrance they could not believe their eyes.

They had made it around the world and now were home again. They could tell their story and how good it was to be back and how they would never leave the home they love so much.

As they walked toward Gus's tree there seemed to be **BLUE RIBBONS** everywhere. Gus thought it must be a gathering of all the squirrels for a meeting. He and Patty would join them and see what it was all about. When Gus and Patty arrived at the group every-one started jumping up and down and making so much noise that Gus had to tell them to

quiet down. Finally, they did.

Freddie told Patty and Gus that they had been away for so long and no one knew what happened to them. They would gather every night wearing their **BLUE RIBBONS**. They hoped someone would tell them they found 2 squirrels wearing **BLUE RIBBONS** and they would bring them home. **BLUE RIBBONS** have always had a special meaning to the squirrels and now they have come home and they would never leave again.

Patty had finished telling her dream to Gus. For a moment he was unable to speak. Then, he told Patty that it was a wonderful but scary dream. He said that he would always take care of her.

He said that all the squirrels would live together forever, with no fear of any of them going away. Gus promised not to tell Patty's dream to anyone. It was their secret. Patty and Gus will always be together safe.

Patty has a Dream tells the story of love and sharing and what home really means. A place to love and be loved always. I hope Patty makes you love her as much as Gus and the other squirrels do.

Gus finds a Way

Illustrated by Kerri Cettei

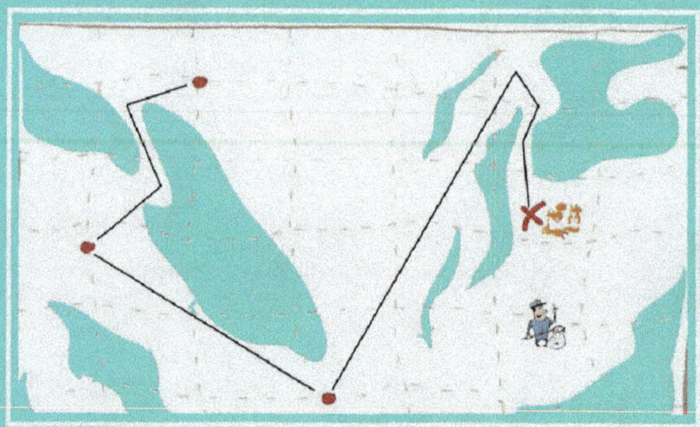

LINDA NELSON

THE BLUE SQUIRREL

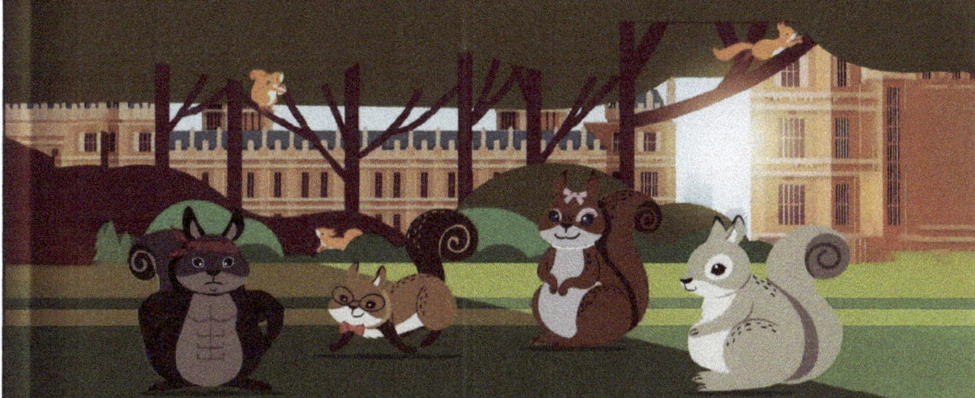

A BOOK BY
LINDA NELSON

The End

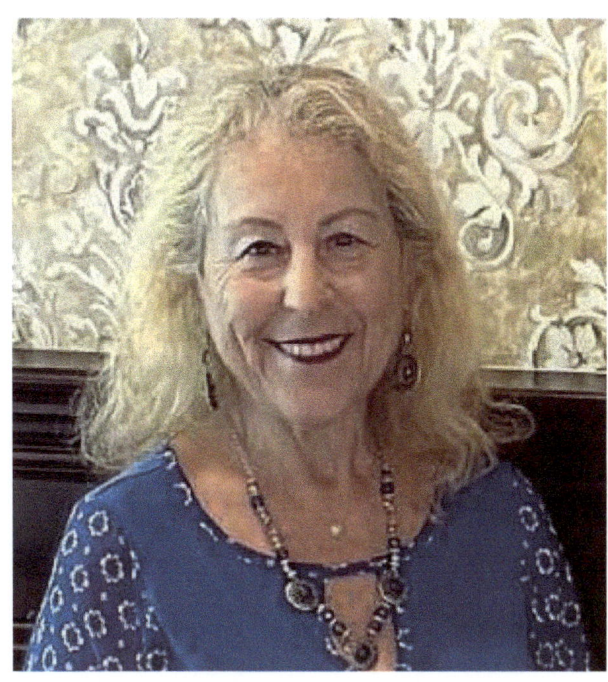

About the Author

Linda Nelson lives on the East End of Long Island, New York and is a graduate of Chamberlayne College in Massachusetts. She has written articles about animals and their behavior in a fictional form for some time. Her inspiration for this book was her love of children and the pleasure that reading brings to a young audience. This Blue Squirrel brings you directly into the adventures of its main character Gus whom you learn to admire and want to read more about.

Presently another sequel is being worked on and hope to be completed by years end.

Illustration done by Kerri Cettel

Gus finds a Way draws the reader into the adventures of Gus and his friends, delightful. My children just loved these books.

Book is very well packaged for giving.

I enjoy reading it to my children before bedtime, a must!

Wonderful book! Very entertaining.

Precious book, my son has read it over and over again, delighted!

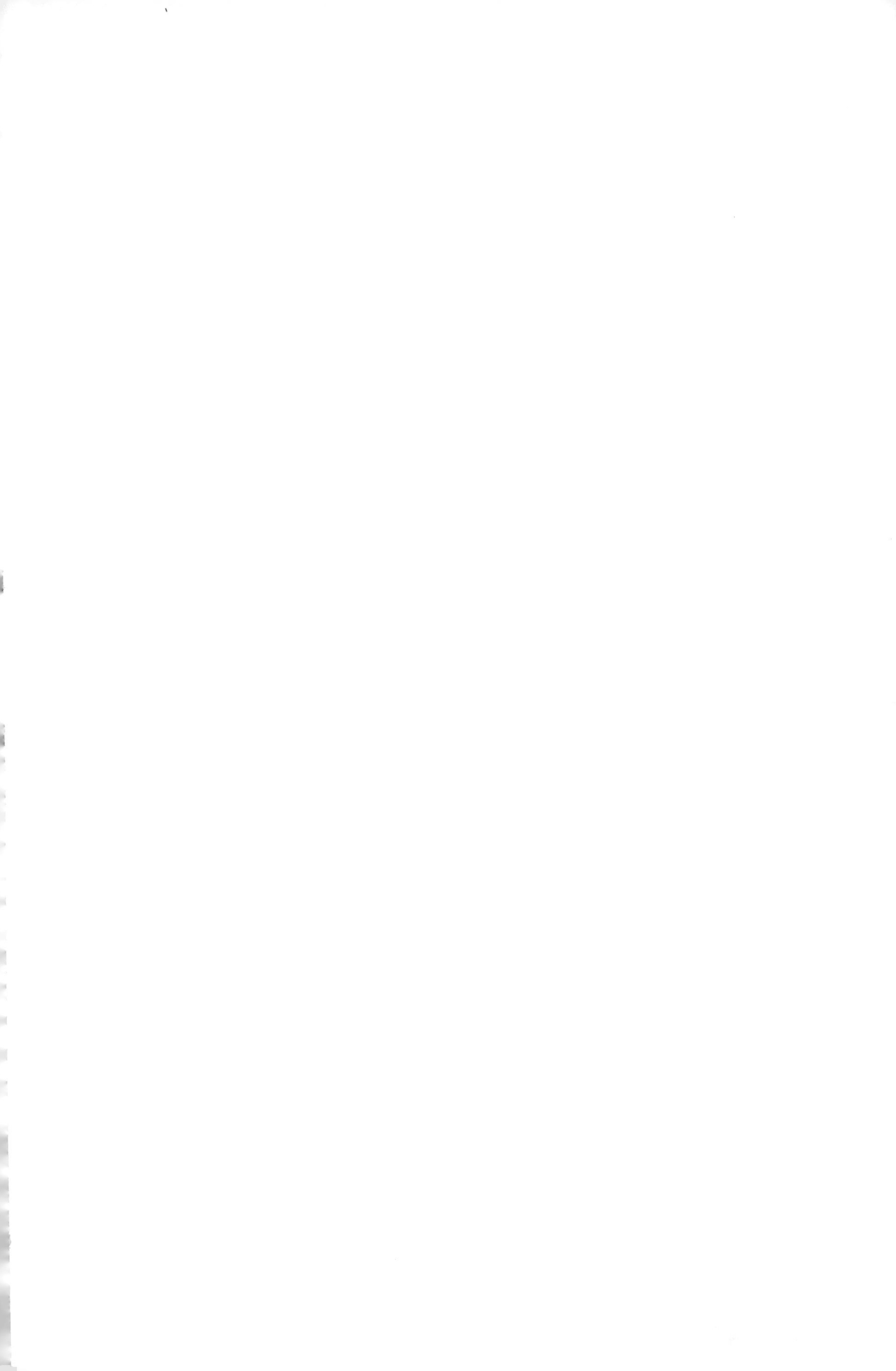

AF400950